PENGUIN CLASSICS

LETTERS FROM A STOIC

ADVISORY EDITOR: BETTY RADICE

LUCIUS ANNAEUS SENECA, statesman, philosopher, advocate and man of letters, was born at Cordoba in Spain around 4 B.C. Despite his relatively undistinguished background and ever-recurrent ill health, he rose rapidly to prominence at Rome, pursuing the double career in the courts and political life for which he had been trained. He began also quickly to acquire celebrity as an author of tragedies and of polished essays, moral, literary and scientific. Sentenced to death by successive emperors (Caligula in A.D. 37 and Claudius in A.D. 41), he spent eight years in exile on the island of Corsica, allegedly for an affair with Caligula's sister. Recalled in A.D. 49, he was made praetor, and was appointed tutor to the boy who was to become, in A.D. 54, the emperor Nero. On Nero's succession Seneca acted for some eight years as an unofficial chief minister. The early part of this reign was remembered as a period of sound imperial government, for which, according to our sources, the main credit must be given to Seneca. His control over an increasingly cruel emperor declined as enemies turned Nero against him with representations that his popularity made him a danger, or with accusations of immorality or excessive wealth ill assorting with the noble Stoic principles he professed. Retiring from public life he devoted his last year or so to philosophy and writing, particularly the *Letters from a Stoic*. In A.D. 65, following the discovery of a plot against the emperor, which might have resulted in Seneca's elevation to the throne, he and many others were compelled by Nero to commit suicide. His name as an essayist and dramatist has recently returned to prominence following two or three centuries of literary oblivion.

ROBIN CAMPBELL lives on the northwest coast of Scotland. He decided that Seneca was overdue for rediscovery while gaining a First in Honour Mods at Wadham College, Oxford. As a Gordon Highlanders officer he had served in Kenya and Uganda with African troops, and after a year at Cambridge learning among other things another Bantu language, he returned to Africa for a few years as a District Officer and, following Zambia's independence as a Magistrate, completed this translation at intervals of leisure in the bush. His later main career as a barrister in Gray's Inn, London, was usually concerned with action by local authorities. He holds strong views on the importance and difficulties of good translation.

SENECA

Letters from a Stoic

Epistulae Morales ad Lucilium

Selected and Translated with an Introduction by
ROBIN CAMPBELL

PENGUIN BOOKS

PENGUIN BOOKS

Published by the Penguin Group
Penguin Books Ltd, 80 Strand, London WC2R 0RL, England
Penguin Group (USA) Inc., 375 Hudson Street, New York, New York 10014, USA
Penguin Books Australia Ltd, 250 Camberwell Road, Camberwell, Victoria 3124, Australia
Penguin Books Canada Ltd, 10 Alcorn Avenue, Toronto, Ontario, Canada M4V 3B2
Penguin Books India (P) Ltd, 11 Community Centre, Panchsheel Park, New Delhi – 110 017, India
Penguin Books (NZ) Ltd, cnr Airborne and Rosedale Roads, Albany, Auckland, New Zealand
Penguin Books (South Africa) (Pty) Ltd, 24 Sturdee Avenue, Rosebank 2196, South Africa

Penguin Books Ltd, Registered Offices: 80 Strand, London WC2R 0RL, England

www.penguin.com

First published 1969
Reprinted with minor revisions 2004

066

Copyright © Robin Alexander Campbell, 1969, 2004
All rights reserved

Printed and bound in Great Britain by Clays Ltd, Elcograf S.p.A.
Set in Monotype Bembo

ISBN-13: 978-0-140-44210-6

www.greenpenguin.co.uk

CONTENTS

INTRODUCTION

SENECA'S LIFE

LUCIUS ANNAEUS SENECA was born at Cordoba, then the leading town in Roman Spain, at about the same time as Christ.[1] His father, Marcus Annaeus Seneca, was an imperial procurator[2] who became an authority on rhetoric, the art of public speaking and debate.[3] He was the father not only of our Seneca, who speaks of his 'old-fashioned strictness',[4] but also of Novatus, later known as Gallio, the governor of Achaea who declined to exercise jurisdiction over St Paul (Acts XVIII, 11–17), and of Mela, less ambitious than his brothers but an able financier (and father of the brilliant young poet Lucan).

Seneca suffered severely from ill health, particularly asthma, throughout his life; he tells us that at one time the only thing which held him back from committing suicide was the thought of his father's inability to bear the loss.[5] He spent a period of his early life in Egypt (where the husband of a devoted aunt named Marcia was the viceroy of the emperor Tiberius from A.D. 16 to 31), there acquiring experience in matters of administration and finance. He also studied the geography and ethnology of Egypt and India[6] and developed a lasting interest in natural science, speculative rather than empirical (although Pliny speaks of him as an authority on geology, marine life and meteorology, and others have admired his remarks on, for example, evolution or the explanation of rings round the sun). His interest was drawn at an early age to Pythagorean mysticism and various cults of eastern origin then gaining adherents in Rome, before his final acceptance, in large part, of the Stoic philosophy.

After training for the bar he took successfully to public life, becoming quaestor in spite of the handicaps of his health, his foreign background and comparative lack of family or other connexions. When Caligula succeeded Tiberius in A.D. 37, Seneca had become a leading speaker in the Senate, and so aroused the jealousy[7] of the new emperor that according to Dio Cassius he ordered his execution and was only induced to let him off by a woman close to the imperial throne who said that Seneca was 'suffering from advanced tuberculosis and it would not be long before he died'.[8] This incident apparently resulted in his temporary retirement from political affairs.

In A.D. 41, in the first year of the reign of Caligula's successor, Claudius, Seneca again came under sentence of death – commuted to banishment – for reasons which we do not know. The pretext was adultery with Julia Livilla, the late emperor's sister; the more likely explanation[9] is that the new ruler's consort, the notorious Messalina, considered him dangerous. His exile on the island of Corsica does not seem to have been endured as stoically as it might have been. The encouraging spirit of an essay of consolation sent to his dearly loved mother Helvia is entirely absent in another addressed to Polybius, an ex-slave who had become a trusted servant of the emperor, which contains some abject flattery and was probably never meant to be published. He had by now suffered the loss not only of his father but of a son, and his first wife died while he was away. The only solace for him in these eight long years of loneliness and near despair was the reception given to the poems, tragedies and essays to friends which he continued composing during his banishment.

His fortunes turned dramatically in A.D. 49. Messalina had been executed and the emperor's new wife, Agrippina, had Seneca recalled to Rome, appointed to the high office of praetor and made tutor to her twelve-year-old son Lucius

Domitius Ahenobarbus (the boy who was shortly to become the emperor Nero). Agrippina's motives, according to Tacitus, apart from the instruction of her son, were a confidence that because of his 'literary fame' the move would gain them popularity, and a belief that he would prove a reliable ally and a useful adviser to herself and Nero in their plans for future power.[10]

There is no evidence that Seneca was connected with the poisoning of Claudius in A.D. 54. But he wrote the speeches which the seventeen-year-old Nero delivered after his accession, and was probably the author of a witty, if to us a little tasteless, attack on the dead ruler's memory (the *Apocolocyntosis* or 'Pumpkinification', an imaginary tale of the rebuffs received by the recently deceased emperor when he presents himself at the portals of Heaven and his application for admission is debated by the Gods). Nero did make a formal speech in honour of his predecessor, which was said to display 'a great deal of polish' and to be a good example of Seneca's 'attractive style, well tuned to the ears of his time'.[11]

The new regime opened well and 'Nero's first five years' were later spoken of as a period of unequalled good government, the emperor Trajan even calling them the finest period in the history of imperial Rome.[12] For this Rome was indebted to Seneca and an army officer named Burrus. These two, 'the most influential as well as the most enlightened of the men who surrounded Nero' (Dio),[13] 'whose wide experience was common knowledge' (Tacitus),[14] prevented the hot-headed young man from carrying out a lot of murders on his accession and aimed at channelling some of his energies into 'permissible pleasures'.[15] Only briefly alarmed by the poisoning of Britannicus and acting throughout in complete harmony they succeeded in keeping public business out of Agrippina's hands and in their own. Tacitus ascribes the secret of the influence of Seneca to 'his tuition of Nero in public speaking, and his engaging manners and high principles', that of Burrus to 'his military responsibilities and austerity of character'.[16]

The two of them 'took over total power, and exercised it, to the utmost of their ability, in the best and justest way conceivable, thus each alike arousing all men's approval' (Dio).[17] While Nero amused himself they set about the problems of government; we notice – to give instances of their activity – legal and financial reforms including the reduction of indirect taxation and steps to prevent peculation and extortion by provincial governors, and the prosecution of a successful war in Armenia to settle the empire's eastern frontier. Seneca's geographical interests appear in the dispatch of an expedition 'to investigate the source of the Nile'. Yet another of his interests was shorthand, the Roman system of which he is said to have completely revised.

Neither he nor Burrus appears to have held any standing legal or constitutional office that could be said to give them the authority they wielded during these years. Seneca, 'the real master of the world',[18] seems simply to have been the moving force behind the throne. It is probably safe to say that Nero (unlike Aristotle's celebrated pupil at a similar age, Alexander the Great) was still under the influence of a teacher of undoubted personal charm, and was quite content to leave to him the direction of affairs in which he had little real interest. Once the young emperor began to listen to other advisers and increasingly to indulge his more violent and vindictive impulses this happy situation was doomed.

In A.D. 58 Seneca was being attacked by people like Publius Suillius Rufus.[19] Accusations seem to have ranged in gravity from sleeping with the emperor's mother (obviously the man had failed to learn his lesson from his 'thoroughly deserved' banishment for 'seducing imperial princesses') and the introduction of the emperor to paederasty, to the uselessness of his studies and the affectedness of his oratorical style. But the campaign against him generally centred on the apparent contrast – it has been a stock criticism of Seneca right down the centuries – between his philosophical teachings and his practice. Instances of this hypocrisy, according to Suillius, were the philosopher's denunciations of tyranny, which did not stop him from being tutor to a tyrant; of flattery, ill according with the attitude he had adopted, especially from exile, towards ex-slaves who headed departments in Claudius' administration; of extravagance, in spite of (allegedly) giving banquets served at five hundred identical tables of citrus wood with ivory legs; and, above all, of wealth. 'What kind of wisdom,' asked Suillius, 'what philosophical teachings, had led him to acquire three hundred million sesterces within the space of four years in royal favour? The childless and their legacies had been, if he might so put it, enticed into Seneca's net, whilst all Italy and the provinces were being sucked dry by his practice of lending money at unlimited rates of interest.'

Seneca was indeed already celebrated for his riches. Juvenal mentions 'the great Gardens of the immensely wealthy Seneca'.[20] Agrippina, says Dio, had acquired for him 'untold wealth from all sources'.[21] The agricultural writer Columella mentions the remarkable productivity of his wine growing estates, the best in Italy, at Mentana.[22] The reply, if any, which Seneca gave to his attackers' criticisms of his wealth, was probably that contained in an essay *On the Happy Life* sent to his brother Gallio. What counts, he says, is one's attitude to wealth, which is the wise man's servant and the fool's master; he, like any good Stoic, could lose all he had at any moment without being a whit less happy. This is the core of a long reply to the charge, which he states with complete frankness, that 'philosophers do not practise what they preach'. His everyday life did not lend countenance to such attacks (we have at least his own accounts[23] of his plain diet and life-long teetotalism, his hard bed, cold baths and daily runs); and on this occasion he came to no harm from his enemies.

In A.D. 59 Nero had his mother put to death, the murder being carried out in cold blood after the calamitous failure of an attempt to stage an accident at sea. There is reason to believe that Seneca and Burrus had no knowledge of or part in the planning of this crime, but as the facts became known did their best to lessen its impact on public opinion. Seneca certainly drafted the letter sent to the Senate 'explaining' how her death was the result of the exposure of a dangerous plot of hers against the emperor's life. Dio would have us believe that Seneca averted a general massacre by saying to Nero, 'However many people you slaughter you cannot kill your successor.'[24]

Tacitus[25] tells us that the death ('probably murder') of Burrus in A.D. 62 'broke Seneca's power'. Enemies gained the ear of Nero with tales of Seneca's popularity and growing wealth; the first was represented as being dangerous to the throne, the second as overshadowing the possessions of the emperor himself (whose abilities as an artist and a speaker were also, it was said, being disparaged by his old instructor). Nero, they said, was now grown up and it was time for him to 'shake off his tutor'. Seneca, warned of this by friends, realized his danger and decided to ask the emperor for permission to retire from public life. The request was eventually granted and the parting was made amicable.

For the last year or so of his life, Seneca devoted himself to philosophy and writing, including the *Epistulae Morales* to Lucilius Junior, a native of Pompeii, a hard-working higher civil servant (procurator in Sicily at the time) who appears to have dabbled in literature and philosophy. Spending his time moving around southern Italy with Paulina, his second wife, Seneca now rarely visited Rome, and even, to disarm suspicion or for greater safety, gave (says Dio) his entire fortune to the emperor. Tacitus mentions a story of an attempt on his life by poisoning, averted either because a slave gave the plot away or because the philosopher was, in fear of just such an attack, living on 'an extremely simple diet of fruits growing wild and running water'.[26]

Then in A.D. 65 came the disastrous conspiracy against the emperor by Piso and others, quite possibly including Seneca. There was a report of a sub-conspiracy to kill Piso as well and make Seneca emperor – 'being a man who seemed to be marked out for supreme power by the good qualities for which he was so famous'.[27] Many people lost their lives on the discovery of the plot. Seneca, like many others, was asked to commit suicide, the then prevailing method of imperial execution. Tacitus' description of his death is not quickly forgotten.[28] His brothers and Lucan followed him, all by their own hands, in the course of Nero's frenzied purge of enemies real and imagined.

According to some, a true Stoic, like Cato under the Republic, would have stayed on in political life to the bitter end. But after the loss of all his influence over Nero, the Spaniard could hardly have hoped to be of useful service any longer to the Roman world, and (in an age in which many lived in recurrent dread of a capricious emperor's message demanding, obliquely or otherwise, the recipient's suicide) the alternative to his retirement was undoubtedly death. Certain other Stoics, indeed, stood up to emperors and were rewarded for their opposition to misrule with martyrdom. Seneca chose to spend what time was left to him in philosophy, and the reader may be left to decide, in fairness not forgetting his chronic ill health, whether his 'lack of moral courage outside the study' in this or earlier events detracts from his achievements. Surprisingly, perhaps, the satirist of the century,

Juvenal, does not pick on the difference between this public figure's conduct and his philosophical professions, of which a variety of later writers have made play.[29] 'Sir, are you so grossly ignorant of human nature,' asked Dr Johnson, 'as not to know that a man may be very sincere in good principles without having good practice?' Seneca, all the same, may well be history's most notable example of a man who failed to live up to his principles.

This does not prevent him from being the outstanding figure of his age. 'Seneca, in those days unsurpassed both in the field of letters and in power (power which afterwards grew too great and recoiled upon his own head), was the last man to be impressed by things which did not count,' said his contemporary Pliny.[30] Money, power or achievements in public life or letters are – despite the interest of the little we know of his career – not the things with which Seneca would want to be connected by people coming across his name today. That he did not expect to be forgotten we know (in one letter he actually promises Lucilius immortality through having corresponded with him); but what he would have liked to be remembered for would have been the value of the ideas which, so he tells Lucilius in his eighth letter, he was committing to writing in the hope that they might be 'of use to later generations'.

SENECA AND PHILOSOPHY

Stoicism, for centuries the most influential philosophy in the Graeco-Roman world, had a long history before Seneca. Founded by Zeno (born of Phoenician descent in Cyprus c. 336/5 B.C.) who had taught or lectured in a well-known *stoa* (a colonnade or porch) – hence the name – in Athens, it had been developed and modified by a succession of thinkers whose opinions on various logical, ethical or cosmological questions showed some fair divergencies. As a moral creed, however, it was based throughout on the following framework of belief.

The Stoics saw the world as a single great community in which all men are brothers, ruled by a supreme providence which could be spoken of, almost according to choice or context, under a variety of names or descriptions including the divine reason, creative reason, nature, the spirit or purpose of the universe, destiny, a personal god, even (by way of concession to traditional religion) 'the gods'. It is man's duty to live in conformity with the divine will, and this means, firstly, bringing his life into line with 'nature's laws', and secondly, resigning himself completely and uncomplainingly to whatever fate may send him. Only by living thus, and not setting too high a value on things which can at any moment be taken away from him, can he discover that true, unshakeable peace and contentment to which ambition, luxury and above all avarice are among the greatest obstacles.

Living 'in accordance with nature' means not only questioning convention and training ourselves to do without all except the necessities (plain food, water, basic clothing and shelter) but developing the inborn gift of reason which marks us off as different from the animal world. We are meant to set free or perfect this rational element, this particle of the universal reason, the 'divine spark' in our human make-up, so that it may campaign against and conquer pain, grief, superstition and the fear of death. It will show us that 'there's nothing either good or bad but thinking makes it so', discipline the pleasures and the passions, and generally subordinate the body and emotions to the mind and soul.

In this way we shall arrive at the true end of man, happiness, through having attained the one and only good thing in life, the ideal or goal called *arete* in Greek and in Latin *virtus* – for which the English word 'virtue' is so unsatisfactory a translation. This, the *summum bonum* or 'supreme ideal', is usually summarized in ancient philosophy as a combination of four qualities: wisdom (or moral insight), courage, self-control and justice (or upright dealing). It enables a man to be 'self-sufficient', immune to suffering, superior to the wounds and upsets of life (often personalized as Fortuna, the goddess of fortune). Even a slave thus armed can be called 'free', or indeed titled 'a king' since even a king cannot touch him. Another example of these 'paradoxes' for which the Stoics were celebrated is one directed at the vanity of worldly possessions: 'the shortest route to wealth is the contempt of wealth.'[31]

This ethic, together with its backing in a system of physics and logic, had first been given shape in the minds of thinkers who, although Greek-speaking, were for the most part not of European descent, coming from places in Asia Minor or the Levant like Tarsus, Cyprus, and Babylon. This does not seem to have reduced the appeal it made to educated Romans when, around the middle of the second century B.C., it first came to their notice. The duties it inculcated – courage and endurance, self-control and self-reliance, upright conduct and just dealing, simple and unluxurious habits, rationality, obedience to the state – were self-evident to many Romans, corresponding quite closely to the traditional idea of *virtus*. The development of the *jus naturae* by the Roman jurists and Posidonius' identification of the Stoic world community or *cosmopolis* with the Roman Empire made its acceptance even easier. At a later date the Stoic view of the ruler (this term including governors, magistrates and administrative officials)[32] as a man whose actions could be criticized, and even as a minister or servant, was to be disliked by emperors, some of whom replied by expelling 'the philosophers'. But Stoics were usually far from hostile to monarchy as such, however openly they declared that rank counted for nothing against the duty of all men, whatever their station, to play their part in life well.

Despite its wide acceptance in educated circles, early Stoicism had a forbidding aspect which went far to explain its failure to influence the masses. There was something unreal or fictional about the *sapiens*, the wise man or philosopher. This ideal figure seemed, from the way the Stoic lecturers talked, to have somehow become perfect in some sudden transformation long ago; gradual self-improvement was hardly discussed. The target it set seemed too high for ordinary men. It stifled and repressed ordinary human emotions in striving after *apatheia*, immunity to feeling; Cato, the great Stoic saint, is reported to have expressed regret at having kissed his wife in a moment of danger. It held that in certain circumstances a man's self-respect might invite, as an act of supreme nobility, his suicide. In pursuing the ideal of *autarkeia*, self-sufficiency, it seemed to make the perfect man a person detached and aloof from his fellows, superior to the world he lived in. Altogether the impression it conveyed, for all its idealism and sincerity, could be cold, dogmatic and unrealistic. Seneca's contribution to ancient philosophy lay in the humanization of this creed, continuing a process begun long before in Rhodes and Rome by Panaetius and Posidonius.

Although Seneca wrote for a relatively narrow circle of educated persons (usually addressing his compositions to a particular friend or relative as if he were that person's special spiritual adviser) his letters and essays show a Stoicism more closely reconciled with the facts and frailty of human nature. The ideal of *apatheia* is much modified. Self-sufficient though he is, the *sapiens* can now have friends and can grieve, within limits, at the loss of one. It has become his duty to be kind and forgiving towards others, indeed to 'live for the other person'.[33] In his way of living he should avoid being ostentatiously different from those he tries to win from moral ignorance. He has to battle like the rest against his failings, in a long and painful progress towards perfection in which all can do with help from above or the inspiration of others' example. Seneca himself, we observe, occasionally makes immodest statements concerning his own progress, but is capable of humility, as in one description of himself as 'a long way from being a tolerable, let alone a perfect human being'.[34]

In statements of man's kinship with a beneficent, even loving god and of a belief in conscience as the divinely inspired 'inner light of the spirit', his attitudes are religious beyond anything in Roman state religion, in his day little more than a withered survival of formal worship paid to a host of ancient gods and goddesses. Christian writers have not been slow to recognize the remarkably close parallels between isolated sentences in Seneca's writings and verses of the Bible.[35] On the other hand the word 'God' or 'the gods' was used by the philosophers more as a time-honoured and convenient expression than as standing for any indispensable or even surely identifiable component of the Stoic system. And the tendency of Stoicism was always to exalt man's importance in the universe rather than to abase him before a higher authority. The hope of immortality was occasionally held out but Seneca does not play on it. To him as to most Stoics virtue was to be looked on as its own reward and vice as its own punishment. The religious hunger of the masses of his day was to be met not by philosophy but by the cults of Isis and Mithras and Christianity.

For the ancient world, then, apart from reviving philosophy in Latin literature, he 'spiritualized and humanized'[36] Stoicism. What of Seneca and modern philosophy? The latter, at least in the universities of the English-speaking world, has for some time been set on a course which he would certainly have condemned; he would not have understood the attention it pays to ordinary language, and some of his letters (for example letter XLVIII) make it clear that it would have come in for a share of his impatience with philosophers (not excluding Stoics) who in his eyes degraded philosophy by wasting their time on verbal puzzles or logical hair-splitting. But more than this, he would have denounced the opinion to which most philosophers, tacitly or otherwise, have come round in the last half-century, that it is no part of the business of philosophy to turn people into better persons, as tantamount to desertion or *lèse-majesté*. His tremendous faith in philosophy as a mistress was grounded on a belief that her end was the practical one of curing souls, of bringing peace and order to the feverish minds of men pursuing the wrong aims in life. 'What we say should be of use, not just entertaining.'[37] Even speculation on the nature or meaning of the universe was of secondary importance, something which the philosopher might or might not, as he chose, take up in leisure moments. A philosopher's words should (as a Quaker might put it) 'speak to our condition'. Fielding's observation that few people in the position of being 'over-loaded with prosperity or adversity' could be too wise or too foolish not to gain from reading Seneca might have gratified him not merely as an indication that his writings were proving 'of use' to later generations, but also as showing that a philosopher could still be regarded as someone to be turned to for advice or consolation. To Seneca, as Letter XC and other letters plainly show, the philosopher and the wise man were the same person.

Whether or not his letters may still be turned to for their pointers to the contented life, they cannot be read without noticing how far in advance of their time are many of his ideas – on the shows in the arena, for example, or the treatment of slaves. His implicit belief in the equality and brother-hood of man despite all barriers of race or class or rank, was one, resurrected from the days of the early Stoics, which led directly to great improvements in the legal position of slaves; besides explaining the then remarkable attitude towards slaves expressed in Letter XLVII, the belief was also the germ of the notion of natural law, the law which was thought to transcend national boundaries and form a basis for the validity of international law. These elements of Stoicism made their not so small or indirect contribution to the French and American revolutions.

SENECA AND LITERATURE

His letters and other writings

'Seneca,' Quintilian tells us, 'turned his hand to practically everything which can be made the subject of study – speeches, poems, letters, dialogues all surviving.' Much of this is lost, including all his speeches (political and forensic), a biography of his father, and essays or treatises on marriage, superstition and a variety of other subjects, mainly scientific.

The works remaining to us (apart from brief poems or epigrams whose attribution to Seneca is sometimes doubtful) are of two main kinds. There are, first, the philosophical letters and essays, including treatises with such titles as *The Happy Life*, *The Shortness of Life*, *Providence*, *Anger*, *Clemency*, *Problems in Natural Science* and literary *consolationes* to persons in bereavement. And secondly there are the tragedies, probably never staged and intended only for reading or recitation among a relatively small circle.[38]

The one hundred and twenty four letters to Lucilius comprise something entirely new in literature. For in these, which were his most conspicuous and immediate literary success, Seneca if anyone is the founder of the Essay. As Francis Bacon put it to Prince Henry in the dedication of his own *Essays*: 'The word is late, but the thing is auncient. For Senecaes Epistles to Lucilius, yf one marke them well, are but Essaies, that is, dispersed Meditacions, thoughe conveyed in the forme of Epistles.' The *Epistulae Morales* are essays in disguise. It has been said[39] that they were real letters edited for publication. It seems most likely that they were intended from the first for publication, possibly preceded by an interval of private circulation. No replies have come down to us.

The atmosphere varies from that of lively, not to say colloquial, conversation to that of the serious treatise; it is occasionally raised to higher levels,[40] but generally remains informal. The 'teaching' is generously eclectic; the first thirty letters each contain some quotation from or reference to writings of the main rival philosophical school, the Epicureans. The introduction of imaginary queries or objections (often scathing in tone) from the correspondent or another interjector and the frequent and urgent exhortation of the listener to self-improvement suggest the atmosphere of the diatribe, while confidences about the writer's own character and the not uncommon choice of consolation or friendship as a theme serve to keep up the air of the letter. Personal happenings or surroundings are regularly made the occasion of, or the preliminary to, serious reflections in the abstract. There are also biting condemnations of ways of life around the writer, particularly among the bored and pleasure-seeking Roman aristocracy. Room is found too for culture, in an assimilable form, in balanced discussions of time-honoured philosophical or ethical problems,[41] or in the development of thoughts on, for example, poetry, or physical phenomena, or style.

*

His style

Style, with Seneca, is of considerable importance. Notwithstanding his own condemnation[42] of people who give less
attention to what they have to say than to *how* they will say
it, he is a signal example of a writer to whom form mattered
as much as content. In writers like him (in what has commonly
been called the Silver Age of Latin literature), constant
striving after terseness and originality of expression gave rise
to an arresting and not easily digested style.

There were reasons for the development of this 'pointed'
style. With the passing of the Republic and succession of a
series of suspicious emperors there had been a diminution
both in the range of subject-matter which was safe and in the
practical value of a training in rhetoric for a career in public
life. The leisured Roman (now increasingly over-leisured)
turned his training to literary rather than political ends; and
the means to the prime new end of stylistic brilliance were
those of rhetoric. All this was encouraged by the fashion of
giving public readings of one's work, in which success almost
came to be measured by the ability of each and every sentence to win applause. Carried over, too, from the schools of
rhetoric was a liking for sometimes daringly poetic words,
especially from Virgil, and artificial forms of expression more
typical of verse than prose.

Going with the overriding aim of pithiness or epigrammatic
brevity (contrasting so greatly with the style of Cicero a
century before) was an indulgence in colloquialisms. Seneca's
use of popular turns of phrase and everyday expressions (a
practice rare in Roman authors not writing for the comic
stage or on technical subjects) and deliberate cultivation of the
easy, conversational manner are somehow reconciled with
elements of style, even in the Letters, which to us seem highly

wrought and polished. The exploitation of such figures as antithesis, alliteration, homeoteleuta and all manner of other plays upon words, paradox and oxymoron, apposition and asyndeton, the use of cases and prepositions in uncommon connotations, all contribute to the twin aims of brevity and sparkle.

The result may read more naturally in Latin than it ever could in English, but is none the less apt to leave the reader 'dazzled and fatigued'.[43] All the wealth and ingenuity of epigram and illustration does not prevent us from feeling that the sentences often simply 'repeat the same thought, clothed in constantly different guises, over and over again', as Fronto complained in the century following. And this reluctance, as it appears, to say what one has to say and then have done with it instead of continuing the restless manufacture of yet bolder, more hard-hitting or more finished sentences or proverbs, sometimes arouses the impatience of more modern readers. There is Macaulay's celebrated statement in a letter to a friend: 'I cannot bear Seneca ... His works are made up of mottoes. There is hardly a sentence which might not be quoted; but to read him straightforward is like dining on nothing but anchovy sauce.' Quintilian[44] considered that Seneca, whom by and large he respected and admired, weakened the force of his teaching by his manner of writing, and others have wondered whether his style is not unworthy of his subject.

It is interesting to hear Quintilian speaking of his struggle to win his students away from such models as Seneca (who, he said, 'practically alone among authors was to be found on the shelves of every young man at that time'). As an academician who stood for orthodoxy and a return to the older or Ciceronian manner, he could not bring himself to give the seal of his approval to an author whose writing showed, in his opinion, 'a degree of corruption all the more dangerous through the very attractiveness of the faults in which it abounds', and who had actually voiced the heresy: 'There are no fixed rules of style.'[45]

*

His influence and appeal

While scholars and schoolmasters in the century following continued to condemn[46] Seneca, early Christians were taking to this kindred spirit among pagan writers, so many of whose ideas and attitudes they felt able to adopt or share. Anthologies were made of him and he was frequently quoted by such writers as Jerome, Lactantius and Augustine. Tertullian called him *saepe noster*, 'often one of us'. The extant set of letters purporting to be correspondence between Seneca and St Paul (probably composed by a Christian, but apparently believed genuine until quite modern times) led Jerome to include him in his so called Catalogue of Saints, and no doubt helps to explain his reputation in the middle ages, much as the supposed prophecy of the birth of the Messiah in Virgil's Fourth Eclogue helped to make the latter's name in Christendom.

Only Cicero, perhaps, among classical authors was better known in medieval times, and until Aristotle was rediscovered by Western Europe, Seneca's main 'scientific' work, the *Naturales Quaestiones*, was the undisputed authority on the subjects with which it dealt. Dante, Chaucer and Petrarch were great admirers and quoters of his writings.[47] Printing spread his influence, the first printed version of the *Epistulae* being published in or about 1475 at Rome, Paris and Strasbourg. Erasmus[48] was the first person to produce a critical edition (in 1515) and Calvin's first work was an edition in 1532 of the *De Clementia*, an essay originally written to encourage clemency in Nero, and incidentally inspiring much of the 'quality of mercy' speech in the Merchant of Venice.

Montaigne[49] was the first, and the most conspicuously indebted, borrower from Seneca among the great modern literary figures. Pasquier's admiration for Montaigne prompted him to say: 'As for his essays, which I call masterpieces, there is no book in my possession which I have so greatly cherished. I always find something in it to please me. It is a French Seneca.'

Appreciations of Seneca as a moralist may be quoted from many sources. John of Salisbury is supposed to have said: 'If Quintilian will excuse my saying so, there are very few if any writers on conduct among non-Christians whose words and ideas can be more readily applied to all kinds of practical things.' Emerson urged: 'Make your own Bible. Select and collect all the words and sentences that in all your reading have been to you like the blast of triumph out of Shakespeare, Seneca, Moses, John and Paul.' He is placed in even more exalted company by Baudelaire in his essay *De l'Essence du Rire*, in which he seems at one point to be ascribing modern civilized manners to '*la venue de Jésus, Platon et Sénèque aidant*'. In letters to Peter Gilles we find Erasmus writing (in the words of Froude) 'in fraternal good humour, advising him to be regular at his work, to keep a journal, to remember that life was short, to study Plato and Seneca, love his wife, and disregard the world's opinion'. Queen Elizabeth I 'did much admire Seneca's wholesome advisings', says her godson, Sir John Harington, who 'saw much of her translating thereof'.[50] Although great literary figures have usually been fondest of the letters, it was his plays which, with all their faults, had the greatest effect on European literature. 'If you seek Seneca's memorial, look round on the tragic stage of England, France and Italy.'[51]

The late Elizabethan age and early seventeenth century

were the high-water mark of Seneca's influence, as a writer well known and imitated among lyric poets and essayists as well as dramatists.[52] His popularity lasted for some time in France, where his admirers included Descartes, Corneille, La Fontaine, Poussin, Rousseau, Diderot, Balzac and Sainte-Beuve. His name disappeared from view for a long period in Britain. The enthusiasm of, for example, De Quincey ('A nobler master of thinking Paganism has not to shew, nor, when the cant of criticism has done its worst, a more brilliant master of composition') was exceptional. It is only recently that the light has been turned on him once more as thinker or as dramatist. The sun shines on a fine statue of him erected in 1965 in Cordoba, and plays of his have reached the stage again in western countries.

NOTE ON TRANSLATION AND TEXT

Translations, and the aims and methods (when they are venturesome enough to profess them) of individual translators, are seldom hard to criticize. But however far men of letters may find themselves from agreement on the principles of translation from a classical author, the intelligent reader can no longer be satisfied with either a literal rendering – on the painful model of the old-fashioned school crib – or an inspired paraphrase – however attractive the result has sometimes been when poet has rendered poet. Somewhere between these two kinds of offering lies the ideal translation, the aim of which I should define as the exact reproduction of the original without omission or addition, capturing its sound (form, style) as well as its sense (content, meaning).

Reproduction of the style presents, except with ordinary conversational or colloquial prose, formidable problems. The practitioner feels that the attempt is one which should be made, even, in the case of poetry, with so difficult a feature of it as its metrical patterns. Yet the result must never be English so unnatural or contrived (unless the original itself clearly set out to obtain such effects) that the reader cannot stomach it. And this consideration has tempered my feeling that the brevity or rhetoric or other elements of Seneca's manner should each be closely imitated. It is hardly possible, for instance, to reproduce the compression of such a sentence as *Habere eripitur, habuisse numquam* or *Magis quis veneris quam quo interest*. In this field of style it is never possible to claim that a translation 'loses nothing' of the qualities of the original.

For when all is said and done a translation of a literary work must be readable. To spare the reader the jars which remind him that he is reading a translation, all but the few timeless versions of the classical authors need to be revised or done afresh perhaps every half century. The same principle incidentally suggests that obscurities (allusions, for example, which only a Latinist would notice or appreciate) may be clarified or removed by slight expansion, and I have adopted this practice very occasionally as an alternative to a distracting reference to a note.

The formal beginning and ending of each letter (*Seneca Lucilio suo salutem* and *Vale*) is omitted. Colloquialisms (including the forms 'it's', 'wouldn't', etc. and the everyday habit of ending sentences with prepositions) will be noticed here and there; they have been used only where Seneca's language is thoroughly colloquial or where he is arguing in the second person with an imaginary interjector.

If an earlier translator has hit on a phrase which one becomes (unwillingly) convinced cannot be bettered, it is surely absurd – the more so if one believes that there is almost always only one best rendering in the language of the translator's day – to proceed with a poorer or less accurate one merely for the sake of originality. I am indebted in this way in a number of places to Gummere and Barker, the translators in the Loeb (1917–25) and Clarendon Press (1932) versions respectively.

The translation, originally based on Beltrami's text (1931), has been brought into line with the Oxford Classical Text (1965) of Mr L. D. Reynolds, to whom I am grateful for help on several points of difficulty. My appreciation is extended also to various friends who may not well recall the help or interest and encouragement at one time or another given by them, and among them to my former tutors Mr T. C. W. Stinton and Mr J. P. V. D. Balsdon, who have rescued me from a number of heresies in the parts of this work which they have seen. My thanks are due also to Dr Michael Grant for permission to reprint from *The Annals of Imperial Rome* (Penguin Books, 1956) his translation of Tacitus' account of Seneca's death.

Of the 124 letters to Lucilius some 40 are translated in this book. Anyone wishing to see the entirety may still be able to find this in print (with a Latin text) in three volumes of the Loeb Classical Library in the old translation by R. M. Gummere of Seneca's Epistles (London and Cambridge, Mass., 1917 to 1925).

It may be asked what criteria have been applied in deciding which letters should be included or omitted. The first has been their interest – as they set out a philosophy and contribute to a picture of a man and of his times. The second has been the avoidance of undue repetition of particular themes or topics of a moralist who tends towards repetitiveness. For similar reasons one or two of the letters have been shortened by the omission of a few passages (at places indicated). My ultimate defence must be the anthologist's plea, or confession, that the choice has been a personal one.

POSTSCRIPT TO INTRODUCTION

It is perhaps hard to resist quoting here (in no way seeking
to disarm criticism!) from the preface and postscript to the
anthology *Seneca's Morals by Way of Abstract* published by Sir
Roger L'Estrange in 1673:

Some other Man, in my Place, would perchance, make you
twenty Apologies, for his want of Skill, and Addreſs, in governing this Affair, but theſe are *Formal*, and *Pedantique
Fooleries*: As if any Man that firſt takes himſelf for a
Coxcomb in his own Heart, would afterwards make himſelf
one in Print too. This *Abſtract*, such as it is, you are extremely welcome to; and I am ſorry it is no better, both for your
ſakes and my own: for if it were written up to the Spirit of
the *Original*, it would be one of the moſt valuable Preſents
that ever any private Man beſtow'd upon the Publick:

Books, *and* Diſhes *have this Common Fate; there was never* any
One, *of* Either *of them, that pleas'd* All Palates. *And, in Truth, it
is a* Thing *as little to be* Wiſh'd *for, as* Expected; *For, an
Univerſal Applauſe is at leaſt Two Thirds of a Scandal. So that though
I deliver up theſe Papers to the Preſs, I invite no Man to the Reading
of them: And, whoſoever Reads, and Repents; it is his Own Fault. To
Conclude, as I made this Compoſition Principally for my Self, ſo it
agrees exceedingly Well with My Conſtitution; and yet, if any Man
has a Mind to take part with me, he has Free Leave, and Welcome.
But, let him Carry this Conſideration along with him, that He's a
very Unmannerly Gueſt, that preſſes upon another Bodies*
Table, *and then Quarrels with his Dinner.*

LETTERS

LETTER II

JUDGING from what you tell me and from what I hear, I feel that you show great promise. You do not tear from place to place and unsettle yourself with one move after another. Restlessness of that sort is symptomatic of a sick mind. Nothing, to my way of thinking, is a better proof of a well ordered mind than a man's ability to stop just where he is and pass some time in his own company.

Be careful, however, that there is no element of discursiveness and desultoriness about this reading you refer to, this reading of many different authors and books of every description. You should be extending your stay among writers whose genius is unquestionable, deriving constant nourishment from them if you wish to gain anything from your reading that will find a lasting place in your mind. To be everywhere is to be nowhere. People who spend their whole life travelling abroad end up having plenty of places where they can find hospitality but no real friendships. The same must needs be the case with people who never set about acquiring an intimate acquaintanceship with any one great writer, but skip from one to another, paying flying visits to them all. Food that is vomited up as soon as it is eaten is not assimilated into the body and does not do one any good; nothing hinders a cure so much as frequent changes of treatment; a wound will not heal over if it is being made the subject of experiments with different ointments; a plant which is frequently moved never grows strong. Nothing is so useful that it can be of any service in the mere passing. A multitude of books only gets in one's way. So if you are unable to read all the books in your possession, you have enough when you have all the books you are able to read.

And if you say, 'But I feel like opening different books at different times', my answer will be this: tasting one dish after another is the sign of a fussy stomach, and where the foods are dissimilar and diverse in range they lead to contamination of the system, not nutrition. So always read welltried authors, and if at any moment you find yourself wanting a change from a particular author, go back to ones you have read before.

Each day, too, acquire something which will help you to face poverty, or death, and other ills as well. After running over a lot of different thoughts, pick out one to be digested thoroughly that day. This is what I do myself; out of the many bits I have been reading I lay hold of one. My thought for today is something which I found in Epicurus (yes, I actually make a practice of going over to the enemy's camp – by way of reconnaissance, not as a deserter!). 'A cheerful poverty,' he says, 'is an honourable state.' But if it is cheerful it is not poverty at all. It is not the man who has too little who is poor, but the one who hankers after more. What difference does it make how much there is laid away in a man's safe or in his barns, how many head of stock he grazes or how much capital he puts out at interest, if he is always after what is another's and only counts what he has yet to get, never what he has already. You ask what is the proper limit to a person's wealth? First, having what is essential, and second, having what is enough.

LETTER III

YOU have sent me a letter by the hand of a 'friend' of yours, as you call him. And in the next sentence you warn me to avoid discussing your affairs freely with him, since you are not even in the habit of doing so yourself; in other words you have described him as being a friend and then denied this in one and the same letter. Now if you were using that word in a kind of popular sense and not according to its strict meaning, and calling him a 'friend' in much the same way as we refer to candidates as 'gentlemen' or hail someone with the greeting 'my dear fellow' if when we meet him his name slips our memory, we can let this pass. But if you are looking on anyone as a friend when you do not trust him as you trust yourself, you are making a grave mistake, and have failed to grasp sufficiently the full force of true friendship.

Certainly you should discuss everything with a friend; but before you do so, discuss in your mind the man himself. After friendship is formed you must trust, but before that you must judge. Those people who, contrary to Theophrastus' advice, judge a man after they have made him their friend instead of the other way round, certainly put the cart before the horse. Think for a long time whether or not you should admit a given person to your friendship. But when you have decided to do so, welcome him heart and soul, and speak as unreservedly with him as you would with yourself. You should, I need hardly say, live in such a way that there is nothing which you could not as easily tell your enemy as keep to yourself; but seeing that certain matters do arise on which convention decrees silence, the things you should share with your friend are all your worries and deliberations. Regard him as loyal, and you will make him loyal. Some men's fear of being deceived has taught people to deceive them; by their suspiciousness they give them the right to do the wrong thing by them. Why should I keep back anything when I'm with a friend? Why shouldn't I imagine I'm alone when I'm in his company?

There are certain people who tell any person they meet things that should only be confided to friends, unburdening themselves of whatever is on their minds into any ear they please. Others again are shy of confiding in their closest friends, and would not even let themselves, if they could help it, into the secrets they keep hidden deep down inside themselves. We should do neither. Trusting everyone is as much a fault as trusting no one (though I should call the first the worthier and the second the safer behaviour).

Similarly, people who never relax and people who are invariably in a relaxed state merit your disapproval – the former as much as the latter. For a delight in bustling about is not industry – it is only the restless energy of a hunted mind. And the state of mind that looks on all activity as tiresome is not true repose, but a spineless inertia. This prompts me to memorize something which I came across in Pomponius. 'Some men have shrunk so far into dark corners that objects in bright daylight seem quite blurred to them.' A balanced combination of the two attitudes is what we want; the active man should be able to take things easily, while the man who is inclined towards repose should be capable of action. Ask nature: she will tell you that she made both day and night.

LETTER V

I VIEW with pleasure and approval the way you keep on at your studies and sacrifice everything to your single-minded efforts to make yourself every day a better man. I do not merely urge you to persevere in this; I actually implore you to. Let me give you, though, this one piece of advice: refrain from following the example of those whose craving is for attention, not their own improvement, by doing certain

things which are calculated to give rise to comment on your
appearance or way of living generally. Avoid shabby attire,
long hair, an unkempt beard, an outspoken dislike of silver-
ware, sleeping on the ground and all other misguided means
to self-advertisement. The very name of philosophy, however modest the manner in which it is pursued, is unpopular
enough as it is: imagine what the reaction would be if we
started dissociating ourselves from the conventions of society.
Inwardly everything should be different but our outward
face should conform with the crowd. Our clothes should not
be gaudy, yet they should not be dowdy either. We should
not keep silver plate with inlays of solid gold, but at the same
time we should not imagine that doing without gold and
silver is proof that we are leading the simple life. Let our
aim be a way of life not diametrically opposed to, but better
than that of the mob. Otherwise we shall repel and alienate
the very people whose reform we desire; we shall make
them, moreover, reluctant to imitate us in anything for fear
they may have to imitate us in everything. The first thing
philosophy promises us is the feeling of fellowship, of belonging to mankind and being members of a community; being
different will mean the abandoning of that manifesto. We
must watch that the means by which we hope to gain admiration do not earn ridicule and hostility. Our motto, as everyone knows, is to live in conformity with nature: it is quite
contrary to nature to torture one's body, to reject simple
standards of cleanliness and make a point of being dirty, to
adopt a diet that is not just plain but hideous and revolting.
In the same way as a craving for dainties is a token of extravagant living, avoidance of familiar and inexpensive dishes
betokens insanity. Philosophy calls for simple living, not for
doing penance, and the simple way of life need not be a
crude one. The standard which I accept is this: one's life
should be a compromise between the ideal and the popular

morality. People should admire our way of life but they should at the same time find it understandable.

'Does that mean we are to act just like other people? Is there to be no distinction between us and them?' Most certainly there is. Any close observer should be aware that we are different from the mob. Anyone entering our homes should admire us rather than our furnishings. It is a great man that can treat his earthenware as if it was silver, and a man who treats his silver as if it was earthenware is no less great. Finding wealth an intolerable burden is the mark of an unstable mind.

But let me share with you as usual the day's small find (which today is something that I noticed in the Stoic writer Hecato). Limiting one's desires actually helps to cure one of fear. 'Cease to hope,' he says, 'and you will cease to fear.' 'But how,' you will ask, 'can things as diverse as these be linked?' Well, the fact is, Lucilius, that they are bound up with one another, unconnected as they may seem. Widely different though they are, the two of them march in unison like a prisoner and the escort he is handcuffed to. Fear keeps pace with hope. Nor does their so moving together surprise me; both belong to a mind in suspense, to a mind in a state of anxiety through looking into the future. Both are mainly due to projecting our thoughts far ahead of us instead of adapting ourselves to the present. Thus it is that foresight, the greatest blessing humanity has been given, is transformed into a curse. Wild animals run from the dangers they actually see, and once they have escaped them worry no more. We however are tormented alike by what is past and what is to come. A number of our blessings do us harm, for memory brings back the agony of fear while foresight brings it on prematurely. No one confines his unhappiness to the present.

LETTER VI

I SEE in myself, Lucilius, not just an improvement but a transformation, although I would not venture as yet to assure you, or even to hope, that there is nothing left in me needing to be changed. Naturally there are a lot of things about me requiring to be built up or fined down or eliminated. Even this, the fact that it perceives the failings it was unaware of in itself before, is evidence of a change for the better in one's character. In the case of some sick people it is a matter for congratulation when they come to realize for themselves that they are sick.

I should very much like, then, to share this all so sudden metamorphosis of mine with you. Doing so would make me start to feel a surer faith in the friendship that exists between us, that true friendship which not hope nor fear nor concern for personal advantage ever sunders, that friendship in which and for which people are ready to die. I can give you plenty of examples of people who have not been lacking a friend but friendship, something that can never happen when mutual inclination draws two personalities together in a fellowship of desire for all that is honourable. Why cannot it happen? Because they know that everything – and especially their setbacks – is shared between them.

You can't imagine how much of an alteration I see each day bringing about in me. 'Send me, too,' you will be saying, 'the things you've found so effectual.' Indeed I desire to transfer every one of them to you; part of my joy in learning is that it puts me in a position to teach; nothing, however outstanding and however helpful, will ever give me any pleasure if the knowledge is to be for my benefit alone. If wisdom were offered me on the one condition that I should keep it shut away and not divulge it to anyone, I should reject it. There is no enjoying the possession of anything valuable unless one has someone to share it with. I shall send you, accordingly, the actual books themselves, and to save you a lot of trouble hunting all over the place for passages likely to be of use to you, I shall mark the passages so that you can turn straight away to the words I approve and admire.

Personal converse, though, and daily intimacy with someone will be of more benefit to you than any discourse. You should really be here and on the spot, firstly because people believe their eyes rather more than their ears, and secondly because the road is a long one if one proceeds by way of precepts but short and effectual if by way of personal example. Cleanthes would never have been the image of Zeno if he had merely heard him lecture; he lived with him, studied his private life, watched him to see if he lived in accordance with his own principle. Plato, Aristotle and a host of other philosophers all destined to take different paths, derived more from Socrates' character than from his words. It was not Epicurus' school but living under the same roof as Epicurus that turned Metrodorus, Hermarchus and Polyaenus into great men. And yet I do not summon you to my side solely for the sake of your own progress but for my own as well, for we shall be of the utmost benefit to each other.

Meanwhile, since I owe you the daily allowance, I'll tell you what took my fancy in the writings of Hecato today. 'What progress have I made? I am beginning to be my own friend.' That is progress indeed. Such a person will never be alone, and you may be sure he is a friend of all.

LETTER VII

You ask me to say what you should consider it particularly important to avoid. My answer is this: a mass crowd. It is something to which you cannot entrust yourself yet without risk. I at any rate am ready to confess my own frailty in this respect. I never come back home with quite the same moral character I went out with; something or other becomes unsettled where I had achieved internal peace, some one or other of the things I had put to flight reappears on the scene. We who are recovering from a prolonged spiritual sickness are in the same condition as invalids who have been affected to such an extent by prolonged indisposition that they cannot once be taken out of doors without ill effects. Associating with people in large numbers is actually harmful: there is not one of them that will not make some vice or other attractive to us, or leave us carrying the imprint of it or bedaubed all unawares with it. And inevitably enough, the larger the size of the crowd we mingle with, the greater the danger. But nothing is as ruinous to the character as sitting away one's time at a show – for it is then, through the medium of entertainment, that vices creep into one with more than usual ease. What do you take me to mean? That I go home more selfish, more self-seeking and more self-indulgent? Yes, and what is more, a person crueller and less humane through having been in contact with human beings. I happened to go to one of these shows at the time of the lunch-hour interlude, expecting there to be some light and witty entertainment then, some respite for the purpose of affording people's eyes a rest from human blood. Far from it. All the earlier contests were charity in comparison. The nonsense is dispensed with now: what we have now is murder pure and simple. The combatants have nothing to protect them; their whole bodies are exposed to the blows; every thrust they launch gets home. A great many spectators prefer this to the ordinary matches and even to the special, popular demand ones. And quite naturally. There are no helmets and no shields repelling the weapons. What is the point of armour? Or of skill? All that sort of thing just makes the death slower in coming. In the morning men are thrown to the lions and the bears: but it is the spectators they are thrown to in the lunch hour. The spectators insist that each on killing his man shall be thrown against another to be killed in his turn; and the eventual victor is reserved by them for some other form of butchery; the only exit for the contestants is death. Fire and steel keep the slaughter going. And all this happens while the arena is virtually empty.

'But he was a highway robber, he killed a man.' And what of it? Granted that as a murderer he deserved this punishment, what have you done, you wretched fellow, to deserve to watch it? 'Kill him! Flog him! Burn him! Why does he run at the other man's weapon in such a cowardly way? Why isn't he less half-hearted about killing? Why isn't he a bit more enthusiastic about dying? Whip him forward to get his wounds! Make them each offer the other a bare breast and trade blow for blow on them.' And when there is an interval in the show: 'Let's have some throats cut in the meantime, so that there's something happening!' Come now, I say, surely you people realize – if you realize nothing else – that bad examples have a way of recoiling on those who set them? Give thanks to the immortal gods that the men to whom you are giving a lesson in cruelty are not in a position to profit from it.

When a mind is impressionable and has none too firm a hold on what is right, it must be rescued from the crowd: it is so easy for it to go over to the majority. A Socrates, a

Cato or a Laelius might have been shaken in his principles by a multitude of people different from himself: such is the measure of the inability of any of us, even as we perfect our personality's adjustment, to withstand the onset of vices when they come with such a mighty following. A single example of extravagance or greed does a lot of harm – an intimate who leads a pampered life gradually makes one soft and flabby; a wealthy neighbour provokes cravings in one; a companion with a malicious nature tends to rub off some of his rust even on someone of an innocent and open-hearted nature – what then do you imagine the effect on a person's character is when the assault comes from the world at large? You must inevitably either hate or imitate the world. But the right thing is to shun both courses: you should neither become like the bad because they are many, nor be an enemy of the many because they are unlike you. Retire into yourself as much as you can. Associate with people who are likely to improve you. Welcome those whom you are capable of improving. The process is a mutual one: men learn as they teach. And there is no reason why any pride in advertising your talents abroad should lure you forward into the public eye, inducing you to give readings of your works or deliver lectures. I should be glad to see you doing that if what you had to offer them was suitable for the crowd I have been talking about: but the fact is, not one of them is really capable of understanding you. You might perhaps come across one here and there, but even they would need to be trained and developed by you to a point where they could grasp your teaching.' For whose benefit, then, did I learn it all?' If it was for your own benefit that you learnt it you have no call to fear that your trouble may have been wasted.

Just to make sure that I have not been learning solely for my own benefit today, let me share with you three fine quotations I have come across, each concerned with something like the same idea – one of them is by way of payment of the usual debt so far as this letter is concerned, and the other two you are to regard as an advance on account. 'To me,' says Democritus, 'a single man is a crowd, and a crowd is a single man.' Equally good is the answer given by the person, whoever it was (his identity is uncertain), who when asked what was the object of all the trouble he took over a piece of craftsmanship when it would never reach more than a very few people, replied: 'A few is enough for me; so is one; and so is none.' The third is a nice expression used by Epicurus in a letter to one of his colleagues. 'I am writing this,' he says, 'not for the eyes of the many, but for yours alone: for each of us is audience enough for the other.' Lay these up in your heart, my dear Lucilius, that you may scorn the pleasure that comes from the majority's approval. The many speak highly of you, but have you really any grounds for satisfaction with yourself if you are the kind of person the many understand? Your merits should not be outward facing.

LETTER VIII

'ARE you, of all people', you write, 'really telling me to avoid the crowd, to retire from the world and find contentment in a good conscience? Where are those Stoic rules of yours that call on a man to die in harness?' Come now, do I really give you the impression that I advocate a life of inactivity? I have only buried myself away behind closed doors in order to be able to be of use to more people. With me no day is ever whiled away at ease. I claim a good part of my nights for study; I have no time for sleep: I just succumb to it, keeping my eyes at their work when they are heavy-lidded and exhausted from lack of rest. I have withdrawn from affairs as well as from society, and from my own affairs in particular: I am acting on behalf of later generations. I am writing down a few things that may be of use to them; I am committing to writing some helpful recommendations, which might be compared to the formulae of successful medications, the effectiveness of which I have experienced in the case of my own sores, which may not have been completely cured but have at least ceased to spread. I am pointing out to others the right path, which I have recognized only late in life, when I am worn out with my wanderings. 'Avoid,' I cry, 'whatever is approved of by the mob, and things that are the gift of chance. Whenever circumstance brings some welcome thing your way, stop in suspicion and alarm: wild animals and fish alike are taken in by this or that inviting prospect. Do you look on them as presents given you by fortune? They are snares. Anyone among you who wishes to lead a secure life will do his very best to steer well wide of these baited bounties, which comprise yet another instance of the errors we miserable creatures fall into: we think these things are ours when in fact it is we who are caught. That track leads to precipices; life on that giddy level ends in a fall. Once, moreover, prosperity begins to carry us off course, we are no more capable even of bringing the ship to a standstill than of going down with the consolation that she has been held on her course, or of going down once and for all; fortune does not just capsize the boat: she hurls it headlong on the rocks and dashes it to pieces. Cling, therefore, to this sound and wholesome plan of life: indulge the body just so far as suffices for good health. It needs to be treated somewhat strictly to prevent it from being disobedient to the spirit. Your food should appease your hunger, your drink quench your thirst, your clothing keep out the cold, your house be a protection against inclement weather. It makes no difference whether it is built of turf or of variegated marble imported from another country: what you have to understand is that thatch makes a person just as good a roof as gold does. Spurn everything that is added on by way of decoration and display by unnecessary labour. Reflect that nothing merits admiration except the spirit, the impressiveness of which prevents it from being impressed by anything.'

If these are the things I'm saying to myself, if these are the things I'm saying to future generations, don't you think I'm doing more good than when I go into court to enter into a recognizance on someone's behalf, or stamp my seal on a will, or lend my assistance by word or action in the Senate to some candidate for office? Those who appear inactive are, believe me, engaged in far more important activity; they're dealing with matters divine and human at the same moment.

But the time has come to make an end, and in accordance with the practice I've started to make some disbursement on this letter's behalf. For this I shall not draw on my own resources. I'm still turning over the pages of Epicurus, and the following saying, one I read today, comes from him: 'To win true freedom you must be a slave to philosophy.' A person who surrenders and subjects himself to her doesn't have his application deferred from day to day; he's emancipated on the spot, the very service of philosophy being freedom.

Quite possibly you'll be demanding to know why I'm quoting so many fine sayings from Epicurus rather than ones belonging to our own school. But why should you think of them as belonging to Epicurus and not as common property? Think how many poets say things that philosophers have said – or ought to have said! Not to mention the tragedians or our native Roman drama (which has a serious element in it as well and stands halfway between comedy and tragedy), think of the quantity of brilliant lines to be found lying about in farces alone! Think of the number of Publilius' verses that really ought to be spoken by actors wearing the tragic buskins instead of barefooted pantomime actors! I'll quote one verse of his which belongs to philosophy, and the same facet of philosophy that I was occupied with just now, a verse in which he proclaims that gifts which chance brings our way are not to be regarded as possessions:

> If you pray a thing may
> And it does come your way,
> 'Tis a long way from being your own.

I recall your expressing the same idea a good deal more happily and succinctly:

> What fortune has made yours is not your own.

And I can't pass over that even happier expression of yours:

> The boon that could be given can be withdrawn.

(This being from your own stock, I'm not debiting it to your account!)

LETTER IX

YOU desire to know whether Epicurus is right in one of his letters in criticizing those who maintain that the wise man is content with himself and therefore needs no friend. This is what Epicurus objects to in Stilbo and those* who believe that the supreme ideal in life is a mind devoid of feeling or as we say *impatiens*. We are bound to involve ourselves in ambiguity if we try to express in a single word the meaning of the Greek term *apatheia* by transferring it straight into our word *impatientia*. For it may be understood in the

* Philosophers of the Cynic school.

opposite sense to the one we wish, with people taking it to signify the man who is unable to endure anything that goes badly for him instead of what we mean by it, the man who refuses to allow anything that goes badly for him to affect him. Consider then whether it might not be preferable to call it a mind that is 'invulnerable' or 'above all suffering'.

The difference here between the Epicurean and our own school is this: our wise man feels his troubles but overcomes them, while their wise man does not even feel them. We share with them the belief that the wise man is content with himself. Nevertheless, self-sufficient though he is, he still desires a friend, a neighbour, a companion. Notice how self-contented he is: on occasion such a man is content with a mere partial self – if he loses a hand as a result of war or disease, or has one of his eyes, or even both, put out in an accident, he will be satisfied with what remains of himself and be no less pleased with his body now that it is maimed and incomplete than he was when it was whole. But while he does not hanker after what he has lost, he does prefer not to lose them. And this is what we mean when we say the wise man is self-content; he is so in the sense that he is able to do without friends, not that he desires to do without them. When I speak of his being 'able' to do this, what I am saying in fact amounts to this: he bears the loss of a friend with equanimity.

Not that he will then be without a friend, for it is his to decide how soon he makes good the loss. Just as Phidias can carve another statue straight away if he loses one, so our wise man with his skill in the art of making friends will fill the place of someone he has lost. I suppose you will want to know how he will be able to make a friend so quickly. Well, I shall tell you (provided we agree that I may make this the moment to pay my debt and square my account so far as this letter is concerned). 'I shall show you,' said Hecato, 'a

love philtre compounded without drug or herb or witch's
spell. It is this: if you wish to be loved, love.'

Great pleasure is to be found not only in keeping up an
old and established friendship but also in beginning and building up a new one. There is the same difference between having
gained a friend and actually gaining a friend as there is between
a farmer harvesting and a farmer sowing. The philosopher
Attalus used to say that it was more of a pleasure to make a
friend than to have one, 'in the same way as an artist derives
more pleasure from painting than from having completed a
picture'. When his whole attention is absorbed in concentration on the work he is engaged on, a tremendous sense of
satisfaction is created in him by his very absorption. There is
never quite the same gratification after he has lifted his hand
from the finished work. From then on what he is enjoying is
the art's end product, whereas it was the art itself that he
enjoyed while he was actually painting. So with our children,
their growing up brings wider fruits but their infancy was
sweeter.

To come back to the question, the wise man, self-sufficient
as he is, still desires to have a friend if only for the purpose of
practising friendship and ensuring that those talents are not
idle. Not, as Epicurus put it in the same letter, 'for the purpose
of having someone to come and sit beside his bed when he is
ill or come to his rescue when he is hard up or thrown into
chains', but so that on the contrary he may have someone by
whose sickbed he himself may sit or whom he may himself
release when that person is held prisoner by hostile hands.
Anyone thinking of his own interests and seeking out friendship with this in view is making a great mistake. Things will
end as they began; he has secured a friend who is going to
come to his aid if captivity threatens: at the first clank of a
chain that friend will disappear. These are what are commonly
called fair-weather friendships. A person adopted as a friend

for the sake of his usefulness will be cultivated only for so long as he is useful. This explains the crowd of friends that clusters about successful men and the lonely atmosphere about the ruined – their friends running away when it comes to the testing point; it explains the countless scandalous instances of people deserting or betraying others out of fear for themselves. The ending inevitably matches the beginning: a person who starts being friends with you because it pays him will similarly cease to be friends because it pays him to do so. If there is anything in a particular friendship that attracts a man other than the friendship itself, the attraction of some reward or other will counterbalance that of the friendship. What is my object in making a friend? To have someone to be able to die for, someone I may follow into exile, someone for whose life I may put myself up as security and pay the price as well. The thing you describe is not friendship but a business deal, looking to the likely consequences, with advantage as its goal. There can be no doubt that the desire lovers have for each other is not so very different from friendship – you might say it was friendship gone mad. Well, then, does anyone ever fall in love with a view to a profit, or advancement, or celebrity? Actual love in itself, heedless of all other considerations, inflames people's hearts with a passion for the beautiful object, not without the hope, too, that the affection will be mutual. How then can the nobler stimulus of friendship be associated with any ignoble desire?

You may say we are not at present concerned with the question whether friendship is something to be cultivated for its own sake. But this, on the contrary, is exactly what needs proving most; for if friendship is something to be sought out for its own sake, the self-contented man is entitled to pursue it. And how does he approach it? In the same way as he would any object of great beauty, not drawn by gain, not out of alarm at the vicissitudes of fortune. To procure friendship only for better and not for worse is to rob it of all its dignity.

'The wise man is content with himself.' A lot of people, Lucilius, put quite the wrong interpretation on this statement. They remove the wise man from all contact with the world outside, shutting him up inside his own skin. We must be quite clear about the meaning of this sentence and just how much it claims to say. It applies to him so far as happiness in life is concerned: for this all he needs is a rational and elevated spirit that treats fortune with disdain; for the actual business of living he needs a great number of things. I should like to draw your attention to a similar distinction made by Chrysippus. The wise man, he said, lacked nothing but needed a great number of things, whereas 'the fool, on the other hand, needs nothing (for he does not know how to use anything) but lacks everything.' The wise man needs hands and eyes and a great number of things that are required for the purposes of day-to-day life; but he lacks nothing, for lacking something implies that it is a necessity and nothing, to the wise man, is a necessity.

Self-contented as he is, then, he does need friends – and wants as many of them as possible – but not to enable him to lead a happy life; this he will have even without friends. The supreme ideal does not call for any external aids. It is home-grown, wholly self-developed. Once it starts looking outside itself for any part of itself it is on the way to being dominated by fortune.

'But what sort of life,' people may say, 'will the wise man have if he is going to be left without any friends when he is thrown into prison or stranded among foreigners or detained in the course of a voyage in distant parts or cast away on some desert shore?' It will be like that of Jove while nature takes her rest, of brief duration, when the universe is dissolved and the gods are all merged in one, finding repose in himself, absorbed in his own thoughts. Such is more or less the way of the wise man: he retires to his inner self, is his own company. So long in fact as he remains in a position to order his affairs according to his own judgement, he remains self-content even when he marries, even when he brings up his children. He is self-content and yet he would refuse to live if he had to live without any human company at all. Natural promptings (not thoughts of any advantage to himself) impel him towards friendship. We are born with a sense of the pleasantness of friendship just as of other things. In the same way as there exists in man a distaste for solitude and a craving for society, natural instinct drawing one human being to another, so too with this there is something inherent in it that stimulates us into seeking friendships. The wise man, nevertheless, unequalled though he is in his devotion to his friends, though regarding them as being no less important and frequently more important than his own self, will still consider what is valuable in life to be something wholly confined to his inner self. He will repeat the words of Stilbo (the Stilbo whom Epicurus' letter attacks), when his home town was captured and he emerged from the general conflagration, his children lost, his wife lost, alone and none the less a happy man, and was questioned by Demetrius. Asked by this man, known, from the destruction he dealt out to towns, as Demetrius the City Sacker, whether he had lost anything, he replied, 'I have all my valuables with me.' There was an active and courageous man – victorious over the very victory of the enemy! 'I have lost,' he said, 'nothing.' He made Demetrius wonder whether he had won a victory after all. 'All my possessions,' he said, 'are with me', meaning by this the qualities of a just, a good and an enlightened character, and indeed the very fact of not regarding as valuable anything that is capable of being taken away. We are impressed at the way some creatures

pass right through fire without physical harm: how much
more impressive is the way this man came through the
burning and the bloodshed and the ruins uninjured and un-
scathed. Does it make you see how much easier it can be to
conquer a whole people than to conquer a single man?
Those words of Stilbo's are equally those of the Stoic. He
too carries his valuables intact through cities burnt to ashes,
for he is contented with himself. This is the line he draws as
the boundary for his happiness.

In case you imagine that we Stoics are the only people who
produce noble sayings, let me tell you something – see that
you put this down to my credit, even though I have already
settled my account with you for today – Epicurus himself,
who has nothing good to say for Stilbo, has uttered a statement quite like this one of Stilbo's. 'Any man,' he says, 'who
does not think that what he has is more than ample, is an
unhappy man, even if he is the master of the whole world.'
Or if you prefer to see it expressed like this (the point being
that we should be ruled not by the actual words used but by the
sense of them), 'a man is unhappy, though he reign the world
over, if he does not consider himself supremely happy.' To
show you, indeed, that these are sentiments of a universal
character, prompted, evidently, by nature herself, you will
find the following verse in a comic poet:

> Not happy he who thinks himself not so.*

What difference does it make, after all, what your position in
life is if you dislike it yourself?

'What about so-and-so,' you may ask, 'who became rich
in such a despicable manner, or such-and-such a person who
gives orders to a great many people but is at the mercy of a
great many more? Supposing they say they are happy, will
their own opinions to this effect make them happy?' It does

* The authorship is not known.

53

not make any difference what a man says; what matters is how he feels, and not how he feels on one particular day but how he feels at all times. But you have no need to fear that so valuable a thing may fall into unworthy hands. Only the wise man is content with what is his. All foolishness suffers the burden of dissatisfaction with itself.

LETTER XI

I HAVE had a conversation with your talented friend. From the very beginning of his talk with me it was apparent what considerable gifts of character and intelligence he possesses. He gave me a foretaste of his capabilities, to which he will certainly live up, for the things he said, caught as he was quite off his guard, were entirely unrehearsed. As he was recovering his self-possession, he could scarcely get over his embarrassment – always a good sign in a young man – so deep had the blush been that suffused his face. This I rather suspect will remain with him even when he has built up his character and stripped it of all weakness – even when he has become a wise man. For no amount of wisdom enables one to do away with physical or mental weaknesses that arise from natural causes; anything inborn or ingrained in one can by dint of practice be allayed, but not overcome. When they face a crowd of people some men, even ones with the stoutest of hearts, break into the sort of sweat one usually sees on persons in an overheated and exhausted state; some men experience a trembling at the knees when they are about to speak; some a chattering of the teeth, a stuttering tongue or stammering lips. These are things which neither training nor experience ever eliminates. Nature just wields her power and uses the particular weakness to make even the strongest

conscious of her. One of these things I well know is a blush,
which has a habit of suddenly reddening the faces of men of
even the most dignified demeanour. It is of course more
noticeable in the young, with their hotter blood and sensitive
complexions; nevertheless seasoned men and ageing men alike
are affected by it. Some men are more to be feared on the
occasions when they flush than at any other time – as if in so
doing they let loose all their inhibitions; Sulla was at his
wildest when the blood had rushed to his visage. No features
were more susceptible than Pompey's: he never failed to
blush in company, and particularly at public meetings. I
remember Fabianus blushing when he appeared to give
evidence before the Senate, and this bashfulness looked
wonderfully well on him. When this happens it is not due to
some mental infirmity, but to the unfamiliarity of some situation or other, which may not necessarily strike any alarm into
inexperienced people but does produce a reaction in them if
they are thus liable through having a natural, physical pre-
disposition to it; certain people have good, ordinary blood
and others just have an animated, lively sort of blood that
comes to the face quickly.

No amount of wisdom, as I said before, ever banishes
these things; otherwise – if she eradicated every weakness –
wisdom would have dominion over the world of nature.
One's physical make-up and the attributes that were one's
lot at birth remain settled no matter how much or how long
the personality may strive after perfect adjustment. One
cannot ban these things any more than one can call them up.
The tokens used to portray embarrassment by professional
actors, those actors who portray emotion, simulate unhappiness
and reproduce for us fear and apprehension, are a hanging
of the head, a dropping of the voice, a casting down of the
eyes and keeping them fixed on the ground; a blush is something they can never manage to reproduce; it is something that

will neither be summoned up nor be told to stay away. Against these things philosophy holds out no remedy and avails one nothing; they are quite independent; they come unbidden, they go unbidden.

My letter calls for a conclusion. Here's one for you, one that will serve you in good stead, too, which I'd like you to take to heart. 'We need to set our affections on some good man and keep him constantly before our eyes, so that we may live as if he were watching us and do everything as if he saw what we were doing.' This, my dear Lucilius, is Epicurus' advice, and in giving it he has given us a guardian and a moral tutor – and not without reason, either: misdeeds are greatly diminished if a witness is always standing near intending doers. The personality should be provided with someone it can revere, someone whose influence can make even its private, inner life more pure. Happy the man who improves other people not merely when he is in their presence but even when he is in their thoughts! And happy, too, is the person who can so revere another as to adjust and shape his own personality in the light of recollections, even, of that other. A person able to revere another thus will soon deserve to be revered himself. So choose yourself a Cato – or, if Cato seems too severe for you, a Laelius, a man whose character is not quite so strict. Choose someone whose way of life as well as words, and whose very face as mirroring the character that lies behind it, have won your approval. Be always pointing him out to yourself either as your guardian or as your model. There is a need, in my view, for someone as a standard against which our characters can measure themselves. Without a ruler to do it against you won't make the crooked straight.

LETTER XII

WHEREVER I turn I see fresh evidence of my old age. I visited my place just out of Rome recently and was grumbling about the expense of maintaining the building, which was in a dilapidated state. My manager told me the trouble wasn't due to any neglect on his part: he was doing his utmost but the house was old. That house had taken shape under my own hands; what's to become of me if stones of my own age are crumbling like that? Losing my temper I seized at the first excuse that presented itself for venting my irritation on him. 'It's quite clear,' I said, 'that these plane trees are being neglected. There's no foliage on them. Look at those knotty, dried-up branches and those wretched, flaking trunks. That wouldn't happen if someone dug round them and watered them.' He swore by my guardian angel he was doing his utmost: in everything his care was unremitting but the poor things were just old. Between you and me, now, I had planted them myself and seen the first leaf appearing on them myself. Then, turning towards the front door, I said: 'Who's that? Who's that decrepit old person? The door's the proper place for him all right – he looks as if he's on the way out. Where did you get him from? What was the attraction in taking over someone else's dead for burial?' Whereupon the man said, 'Don't you recognize me? I'm Felicio. You used to bring me toy figures.* I'm the son of the manager Philositus, your pet playmate.' 'The man's absolutely crazy,' I said. 'Become a little child again, has he, actually calls himself my playmate? Well, the way he's losing his teeth at this very moment, it's perfectly possible.'

So I owe it to this place of mine near town that my old

* Presents which were customary during the Saturnalia holidays.

age was made clear to me at every turn. Well, we should cherish old age and enjoy it. It is full of pleasure if you know how to use it. Fruit tastes most delicious just when its season is ending. The charms of youth are at their greatest at the time of its passing. It is the final glass which pleases the inveterate drinker, the one that sets the crowning touch on his intoxication and sends him off into oblivion. Every pleasure defers till its last its greatest delights. The time of life which offers the greatest delight is the age that sees the downward movement – not the steep decline – already begun; and in my opinion even the age that stands on the brink has pleasures of its own – or else the very fact of not experiencing the want of any pleasures takes their place. How nice it is to have outworn one's desires and left them behind!

'It's not very pleasant, though,' you may say, 'to have death right before one's eyes.' To this I would say, firstly, that death ought to be right there before the eyes of a young man just as much as an old one – the order in which we each receive our summons is not determined by our precedence in the register – and, secondly, that no one is so very old that it would be quite unnatural for him to hope for one more day....*

Every day, therefore, should be regulated as if it were the one that brings up the rear, the one that rounds out and completes our lives. Pacuvius, the man who acquired a right to Syria by prescription,[53] was in the habit of conducting a memorial ceremony for himself with wine and funeral feasting of the kind we are familiar with, and then being carried on a bier from the dinner table to his bed, while a chanting to music went on of the words 'He has lived, he has lived' in Greek, amid the applause of the young libertines present. Never a day passed but he celebrated his own funeral. What

* A short, obscure digression (§§6 to 7) concerning divisions of time is omitted.

he did from discreditable motives we should do from honourable ones, saying in all joyfulness and cheerfulness as we retire to our beds,

> I have lived; I have completed now the course
> That fortune long ago allotted me.*

If God adds the morrow we should accept it joyfully. The man who looks for the morrow without worrying over it knows a peaceful independence and a happiness beyond all others. Whoever has said 'I have lived' receives a windfall every day he gets up in the morning.

But I must close this letter now. 'What!' you'll be saying. 'Is it coming to me just as it is, without any parting contribution?' Don't worry, it's bringing you something. Why did I call it 'something', though? It's a great deal. For what could be more splendid than the following saying which I'm entrusting to this letter of mine for delivery to you: 'To live under constraint is a misfortune, but there is no constraint to live under constraint.' Of course not, when on every side there are plenty of short and easy roads to freedom there for the taking. Let us thank God that no one can be held a prisoner in life – the very constraints can be trampled under foot.

'It was Epicurus who said that,' you protest. 'What business have you got with someone else's property?' Whatever is true is my property. And I shall persist in inflicting Epicurus on you, in order to bring it home to the people who take an oath of allegiance to someone and never afterwards consider what is being said but only who said it, that the things of greatest merit are common property.

* Virgil, *Aeneid*, IV:653.

LETTER XV

OUR ancestors had a custom, observed right down as far as my own lifetime, of adding to the opening words of a letter: 'I trust this finds you as it leaves me, in good health.' We have good reason to say: 'I trust this finds you in pursuit of wisdom.' For this is precisely what is meant by good health. Without wisdom the mind is sick, and the body itself, however physically powerful, can only have the kind of strength that is found in persons in a demented or delirious state. So this is the sort of healthiness you must make your principal concern. You must attend to the other sort as well, but see that it takes second place. It won't cost you any great trouble if good health is all you want. For it is silly, my dear Lucilius, and no way for an educated man to behave, to spend one's time exercising the biceps, broadening the neck and shoulders and developing the lungs. Even when the extra feeding has produced gratifying results and you've put on a lot of muscle, you'll never match the strength or the weight of a prize ox. The greater load, moreover, on the body is crushing to the spirit and renders it less active. So keep the body within bounds as much as you can and make room for the spirit. Devotees of physical culture have to put up with a lot of nuisances. There are the exercises, in the first place, the toil involved in which drains the vitality and renders it unfit for concentration or the more demanding sort of studies. Next there is the heavy feeding, which dulls mental acuteness. Then there is the taking on as coaches of the worst brand of slave, persons who divide their time between putting on lotion and putting down liquor, whose idea of a well spent day consists of getting up a good sweat and then replacing the fluid lost with plenty of drink, all the better to be absorbed on a dry stomach. Drinking and perspiring – it's the life of a dyspeptic! There are short and simple exercises which will tire the body without undue delay and save what needs especially close accounting for, time. There is running, swinging weights about and jumping – either high-jumping or long-jumping or the kind indulged in by the priests of Mars, if one may so describe it, or to be rather more disrespectful, by the laundress. Pick out any of these for ease and straightforwardness. But whatever you do, return from body to mind very soon. Exercise it day and night. Only a moderate amount of work is needed for it to thrive and develop. It is a form of exercise to which cold and heat and even old age are no obstacle. Cultivate an asset which the passing of time itself improves.

I'm not telling you to be always bent over book or writing-tablets. The mind has to be given some time off, but in such a way that it may be refreshed, not relaxed till it goes to pieces. Travelling in one's carriage shakes the body up and doesn't interfere with intellectual pursuits; you can read, dictate, speak, or listen – nor does walking, for that matter, preclude any of these activities. Nor need you look down on voice-training, though I will not have you practising any of this ascending and then descending again by degrees through set scales – if you start that, you'll be going on to take lessons in walking! Once let into your house the sort of person that hunger teaches unheard-of occupations and you'll have someone regulating the way you walk and watching the way you use your jaws as you eat, and in fact going just as far as your patience and credulity lead his audacity on. Are you to conclude from what I've just said that your voice should start its exercises with immediate shouting at full force? The natural thing is to lead up to it through easy stages, so natural in fact that even persons involved in a quarrel begin in conversational tones: only later do they go on to rend the air. No 'one makes an impassioned appeal for 'the help and support of all true men of Rome' at the very outset. . . .* Our purpose in all this is not to give the voice exercise, but to make it give us exercise.

I have relieved you, then, of no little bother. To these favours there shall be added the following small contribution, a striking maxim that comes from Greece. Here it is: 'The life of folly is empty of gratitude, full of anxiety: it is focused wholly on the future.' 'Who said that?' you ask. The same man as before. And what sort of life do you think is meant by 'the life of folly'? Baba's and Isio's?† No, he means our own life, precipitated by blind desire into activities that are likely to bring us harm and will certainly never bring us satisfaction – if they could ever satisfy us they would have done so by now – never thinking how pleasant it is to ask for nothing, how splendid it is to be complete and be independent of fortune. So continually remind yourself, Lucilius, of the many things you have achieved. When you look at all the people out in front of you, think of all the ones behind you. If you want to feel appreciative where the gods and your life are concerned, just think how many people you've outdone. Why be concerned about others, come to that, when you've outdone your own self? Set yourself a limit which you couldn't even exceed if you wanted to, and say good-bye at last to those deceptive prizes more precious to those who hope for them than to those who have won them. If there were anything substantial in them they would sooner or later bring a sense of fullness; as it is they simply aggravate the thirst of those who swallow them. Away with pomp and show; as for the uncertain lot that the future has in store for me, why should I demand from

* The next sentence (dealing further with the correct manner of declamation) is omitted, the text being hopelessly corrupt.

† Baba, and one may presume also Isio, was a celebrated fool or clown.

fortune that she should give me this and that rather than demand from myself that I should not ask for them? Why should I ask for them, after all? Am I to pile them up in total forgetfulness of the frailty of human existence? What is the purpose of my labours going to be? See, this day's my last – or maybe it isn't, but it's not so far away from it.

LETTER XVI

IT is clear to you, I know, Lucilius, that no one can lead a happy life, or even one that is bearable, without the pursuit of wisdom, and that the perfection of wisdom is what makes the happy life, although even the beginnings of wisdom make life bearable. Yet this conviction, clear as it is, needs to be strengthened and given deeper roots through daily reflection; making noble resolutions is not as important as keeping the resolutions you have made already. You have to persevere and fortify your pertinacity until the will to good becomes a disposition to good. So you needn't go in for all this long-winded protestation or say any more on the subject – I'm well aware that you've made a great deal of progress. I realize the feelings that prompt you to put these things in your letter, and there is no pretence or speciousness about them. But – to give you my honest opinion – at this stage, although I have great hopes of you, I do not yet feel quite confident about you. And I should like you to adopt the same attitude: you've no grounds for forming a ready, hasty belief in yourself. Carry out a searching analysis and close scrutiny of yourself in all sorts of different lights. Consider above all else whether you've advanced in philosophy or just in actual years.

Philosophy is not an occupation of a popular nature, nor

is it pursued for the sake of self-advertisement. Its concern is not with words, but with facts. It is not carried on with the object of passing the day in an entertaining sort of way and taking the boredom out of leisure. It moulds and builds the personality, orders one's life, regulates one's conduct, shows one what one should do and what one should leave undone, sits at the helm and keeps one on the correct course as one is tossed about in perilous seas. Without it no one can lead a life free of fear or worry. Every hour of the day countless situations arise that call for advice, and for that advice we have to look to philosophy.

Someone may say: 'What help can philosophy be to me if there is such a thing as fate? What help can philosophy be if there is a deity controlling all? What help can it be if all is governed by chance? For it is impossible either to change what is already determined or to make preparations to meet what is undetermined; either, in the first case, my planning is forestalled by a God who decrees how I am to act, or, in the second case, it is fortune that allows me no freedom to plan.' Whichever of these alternatives, Lucilius, is true – even if all of them are true – we still need to practise philosophy. Whether we are caught in the grasp of an inexorable law of fate, whether it is God who as lord of the universe has ordered all things, or whether the affairs of mankind are tossed and buffeted haphazardly by chance, it is philosophy that has the duty of protecting us. She will encourage us to submit to God with cheerfulness and to fortune with defiance; she will show you how to follow God and bear what chance may send you. But I mustn't pass on here to a discussion of the problem what is within our control if there is a governing providence, whether we are carried along enmeshed in a train of fated happenings, or whether we are at the mercy of the sudden and the unforeseeable. For the present I go back to the point where I was before, to advise and urge you not to allow your spiritual enthusiasm to cool off or fall away. Keep a hold on it and put it on a firm footing, so that what is at present an enthusiasm may become a settled spiritual disposition.

If I know you, you'll have been looking around from the very start of this letter to see what it's going to bring you by way of a little present. Search the letter and you'll find it. You needn't think my kindness all that remarkable: I am only being generous, still, with someone else's property. Why, though, do I call it someone else's? Whatever is well said by anyone belongs to me. Here is another saying of Epicurus: 'If you shape your life according to nature, you will never be poor; if according to people's opinions, you will never be rich.' Nature's wants are small, while those of opinion are limitless. Imagine that you've piled up all that a veritable host of rich men ever possessed, that fortune has carried you far beyond the bounds of wealth so far as any private individual is concerned, building you a roof of gold and clothing you in royal purple, conducting you to such a height of opulence and luxury that you hide the earth with marble floors – putting you in a position not merely to own, but to walk all over treasures – throw in sculptures, paintings, all that has been produced at tremendous pains by all the arts to satisfy extravagance: all these things will only induce in you a craving for even bigger things. Natural desires are limited; those which spring from false opinions have nowhere to stop, for falsity has no point of termination. When a person is following a track, there is an eventual end to it somewhere, but with wandering at large there is no limit. So give up pointless, empty journeys, and whenever you want to know whether the desire aroused in you by something you are pursuing is natural or quite unseeing, ask yourself whether it is capable of coming to rest at any point; if after going a long way there is always something remaining farther away, be sure it is not something natural.

LETTER XVIII

It is the month of December, and yet the whole city is in a sweat! Festivity at state expense is given unrestricted licence. Everywhere there echoes the noise of preparations on a massive scale. It all suggests that the Saturnalia* holidays are different from the ordinary working day, when the difference is really non-existent – so much so in fact that the man who said that December used to be a month but is now a year was, in my opinion, not far wide of the mark!

If I had you with me I should enjoy consulting you and finding out what course you think we should follow: should we make no alteration in our daily habits, or should we take off our togas – time was when a change from formal wear would come about only during periods of grave political upheaval, whereas with us it happens for holidays' and pleasure's sake! – and have dinner parties with a note of gaiety about them, to avoid giving the impression that we disagree with the ways of those around us? If I know you as well as I think I do and you had to give a decision in the matter, you would say that we should be neither altogether like nor altogether unlike the festive-hatted crowd. But perhaps this is the very season when we should be keeping the soul under strict control, making it unique in abstaining from pleasure just when the crowd are all on pleasure bent. If the soul succeeds in avoiding either heading or being carried away in the direction of the temptations that lead people into extravagant living, no surer proof of its strength of purpose can be vouchsafed it. Remaining dry and sober takes a good deal more strength of will when everyone about one is puking drunk; it takes a more developed sense of fitness, on the other

* A festival lasting several days, commencing on the 17th December.

hand, not to make of oneself a person apart, to be neither indistinguishable from those about one nor conspicuous by one's difference, to do the same things but not in quite the same manner. For a holiday can be celebrated without extravagant festivity.

Still, my determination to put your moral strength of purpose to the test is such that I propose to give even you the following direction found in great men's teaching: set aside now and then a number of days during which you will be content with the plainest of food, and very little of it, and with rough, coarse clothing, and will ask yourself, 'Is this what one used to dread?' It is in times of security that the spirit should be preparing itself to deal with difficult times; while fortune is bestowing favours on it then is the time for it to be strengthened against her rebuffs. In the midst of peace the soldier carries out manoeuvres, throws up earthworks against a non-existent enemy and tires himself out with unnecessary toil in order to be equal to it when it is necessary. If you want a man to keep his head when the crisis comes you must give him some training before it comes. This was the aim of the men* who once every month pretended they were poor, bringing themselves face to face with want, to prevent their ever being terrified by a situation which they had frequently rehearsed.

You must not at this point imagine that I mean meals like Timon's or 'the poor man's room' or anything else to which the extravagance of wealth resorts to amuse away its tedium. That pallet must be a real one, and the same applies to your smock, and your bread must be hard and grimy. Endure all this for three or four days at a time, sometimes more, so that it is a genuine trial and not an amusement. At the end of it, believe me, Lucilius, you will revel in being sated for a

---

* Epicureans. As the next sentence indicates, rich men sometimes had a room fitted out for the purpose.

penny, and will come to see that security from care is not dependent on fortune – for even when she is angry she will always let us have what is enough for our needs.

There is no reason, mind you, why you should suppose yourself to be performing a considerable feat in doing this – you will only be doing something done by thousands upon thousands of slaves and paupers. But take credit on one account, that you will be doing it of your own free choice – and finding it no more difficult to endure on a permanent basis than to try out once in a while. We should be practising with a dummy target, getting to be at home with poverty so that fortune cannot catch us unprepared. We shall be easier in our minds when rich if we have come to realize how far from burdensome it is to be poor. The great hedonist teacher Epicurus used to observe certain periods during which he would be niggardly in satisfying his hunger, with the object of seeing to what extent, if at all, one thereby fell short of attaining full and complete pleasure, and whether it was worth going to much trouble to make the deficit good. At least so he says in the letter he wrote to Polyaenus in the year Charinus was in office. He boasts in it indeed that he is managing to feed himself for less than a halfpenny whereas Metrodorus, not yet having made such good progress, needs a whole half-penny! Do you think such fare can do no more than fill a person up? It can fill him with pleasure as well, and not the kind of insubstantial, fleeting pleasure that needs constant renewal but a pleasure which is sure and lasting. Barley porridge, or a crust of barley bread, and water do not make a very cheerful diet, but nothing gives one keener pleasure than the ability to derive pleasure even from that – and the feeling of having arrived at something which one cannot be deprived of by any unjust stroke of fortune. Prison rations are more generous: the man in the condemned cell is not so scantily fed as that by the executioner; to reduce oneself, then, of

one's own free choice to a diet that no man has any real call
to be apprehensive about even if he is sentenced to death,
that is an act of real spiritual greatness. To do this is truly to
forestall the blows of fortune. So, my dear Lucilius, start
following these men's practice and appoint certain days on
which to give up everything and make yourself at home with
next to nothing. Start cultivating a relationship with poverty.

> Dear guest, be bold enough to pay no heed
> To riches, and so make yourself, like him,
> Worthy of a god.*

For no one is worthy of a god unless he has paid no heed to
riches. I am not, mind you, against your possessing them, but
I want to ensure that you possess them without tremors; and
this you will only achieve in one way, by convincing yourself that you can live a happy life even without them, and by
always regarding them as being on the point of vanishing.

But it's time I started folding up this letter. 'Not till you've
settled your account,' you say. Well, I'll refer you to Epicurus
for payment. 'Anger carried to excess begets madness.' How
true this is you're bound to know, having had both slaves and
enemies. It is a passion, though, which flares up against all
types of people. It is born of love as well as hate, and is as
liable to arise in the course of sport or jesting as in affairs of a
serious kind. The factor that counts is not the importance of the
cause from which it springs but the kind of personality it
lands in, in the same way as with fire what matters is not the
fierceness of the flame but where it catches – solid objects
may resist the fiercest flame while, conversely, dry and in-
flammable matter will nurse a mere spark into a conflagration. It is true, my dear Lucilius. The outcome of violent
anger is a mental raving, and therefore anger is to be avoided
not for the sake of moderation but for the sake of sanity.

* Virgil, *Aeneid*, VIII: 364–5.

LETTER XXVI

It's only a short time since I was telling you I was in sight of old age. Now I'm afraid I may have left old age behind me altogether. Some other term would be more in keeping now with my years, or at least my present physical state, since old age connotes a period of decline, not debility. Put me in the list of the decrepit, the ones on the very brink! However, I congratulate myself, mind you, on the fact that my age has not, so far as I'm aware, brought any deterioration in my spirit, conscious as I am of the deterioration in my constitution. Only my vices and their accessories have decayed: the spirit is full of life, and delighted to be having only limited dealings with the body. It has thrown off a great part of its burden. It's full of vigour, and carrying on an argument with me on the subject of old age, maintaining that these are its finest years. Let's accept what it says, and let it make the most of its blessings. It tells me to start thinking and examine how far I owe this serenity and sobriety to philosophy, and how far I owe it simply to my years, and to investigate with some care what things I really am refusing to do and what I'm simply incapable of doing – and it's prepared to accept whatever I'm really pleased to find myself incapable of doing as equivalent to refusing to do them; and what cause can there be for complaint, after all, in anything that was always bound to come to an end fading gradually away? What is troubling about that? 'Nothing,' you may say, 'could be more troubling than the idea of our wasting and perishing away – melting out of existence, one may aptly call it, since we aren't struck down all of a sudden but worn away, every day that passes diminishing in some degree our powers.' Moving to one's end through nature's own gentle process of dissolution – is there a better way of leaving life than that? Not because there is anything wrong with a sudden, violent departure, but because this gradual withdrawal is an easy route.

Anyway, here's what I do: I imagine to myself that the testing time is drawing near, that the day that is going to see judgement pronounced on the whole of my past life has actually arrived, and I take a look at myself and address myself in these terms: 'All that I've done or said up to now counts for nothing. My showing to date, besides being heavily varnished over, is of paltry value and reliability as a guarantee of my spirit. I'm going to leave it to death to settle what progress I've made. Without anxiety, then, I'm making ready for the day when the tricks and disguises will be put away and I shall come to a verdict on myself, determining whether the courageous attitudes I adopt are really felt or just so many words, and whether or not the defiant challenges I've hurled at fortune have been mere pretence and pantomime. Away with the world's opinion of you – it's always unsettled and divided. Away with the pursuits that have occupied the whole of your life – death is going to deliver the verdict in your case. Yes, all your debates and learned conferences, your scholarly talk and collection of maxims from the teachings of philosophers, are in no way indicative of genuine spiritual strength. Bold words come even from the timidest. It's only when you're breathing your last that the way you've spent your time will become apparent. I accept the terms, and feel no dread of the coming judgement.' That's what I say to myself, but assume that I've said it to you as well. You're younger than I am, but what difference does that make? No count is taken of years. Just where death is expecting you is something we cannot know; so, for your part, expect him everywhere.

I was just intending to stop, my hand considering its closing sentence, but the accounts have still to be made out and this letter issued with its travelling expenses! You may assume that I won't be announcing the source I intend borrowing from – you know whose funds I'm drawing on! Give me a fraction more time and payment will be made out of my own pocket. In the meantime Epicurus will oblige me, with the following saying: 'Rehearse death', or – the idea may come across to us rather more satisfactorily if put in this form – 'It is a very good thing to familiarize oneself with death.' You may possibly think it unnecessary to learn something which you will only have to put into practice once. That is the very reason why we ought to be practising it. We must needs continually study a thing if we are not in a position to test whether we know it. 'Rehearse death.' To say this is to tell a person to rehearse his freedom. A person who has learned how to die has unlearned how to be a slave. He is above, or at any rate beyond the reach of, all political powers. What are prisons, warders, bars to him? He has an open door. There is but one chain holding us in fetters, and that is our love of life. There is no need to cast this love out altogether, but it does need to be lessened somewhat so that, in the event of circumstances ever demanding this, nothing may stand in the way of our being prepared to do at once what we must do at some time or other.

LETTER XXVII

'So you're giving me advice, are you?' you say. 'Have you already given yourself advice, then? Have you already put yourself straight? Is that how you come to have time for reforming other people?' No, I'm not so shameless as to set about treating people when I'm sick myself. I'm talking to you as if I were lying in the same hospital ward, about the

illness we're both suffering from, and passing on some remedies. So listen to me as if I were speaking to myself. I'm
allowing you access to my inmost self, calling you in to advise
me as I have things out with myself. I proclaim to my own
self: 'Count your years and you'll be ashamed to be wanting
and working for exactly the same things as you wanted when
you were a boy. Of this one thing make sure against your
dying day – that your faults die before you do. Have done
with those unsettled pleasures, which cost one dear – they do
one harm after they're past and gone, not merely when they're
in prospect. Even when they're over, pleasures of a depraved
nature are apt to carry feelings of dissatisfaction, in the same
way as a criminal's anxiety doesn't end with the commission
of the crime, even if it's undetected at the time. Such pleasures
are insubstantial and unreliable; even if they don't do one
any harm, they're fleeting in character. Look around for
some enduring good instead. And nothing answers this
description except what the spirit discovers for itself within
itself. A good character is the only guarantee of everlasting,
carefree happiness. Even if some obstacle to this comes on the
scene, its appearance is only to be compared to that of clouds
which drift in front of the sun without ever defeating its
light.'

How soon will you be fortunate enough to attain to this
happiness? Well, you haven't been dragging your steps up
till now, but your pace could be increased. There's a lot of
work remaining to be done, and if you want to be successful
you must devote all your waking hours and all your efforts
to the task personally. This is not something that admits of
delegation. It is a different branch of learning which has room
for devilling. There was a rich man called Calvisius Sabinus, in
my own lifetime, who had a freedman's brains along with a
freedman's fortune. I have never seen greater vulgarity in a
successful man. His memory was so bad that at one moment

or another the names of Ulysses, or Achilles, or Priam,
characters he knew as well as we knew our early teachers,
would slip his memory. No doddering butler ever went
through the introductions of a mass of callers committing
quite such solecisms – not announcing people's names so
much as foisting names on them – as Sabinus did with the
Greek and Trojan heroes. But this didn't stop him wanting to
appear a well-read man. And to this end he thought up the
following short cut: he spent an enormous amount of
money on slaves, one of them to know Homer by heart,
another to know Hesiod, while he assigned one apiece to
each of the nine lyric poets.* That the cost was enormous is
hardly surprising: not having found what he wanted in the
market he had them made to order. After this collection of
slaves had been procured for him, he began to give his
dinner guests nightmares. He would have these fellows at
his elbow so that he could continually be turning to them for
quotations from these poets which he might repeat to the
company, and then – it happened frequently – he would
break down halfway through a word. Satellius Quadratus,
who regarded stupid millionaires as fair game to be sponged
off, and consequently also fair game for flattery, as well as –
and this goes with the other two things – fair game for
facetiousness at their expense, suggested to him that he
should keep a team of scholars 'to pick up the bits'. On
Sabinus' letting it be known that the slaves had set him back
a hundred thousand sesterces apiece, he said: 'Yes, for less
than that you could have bought the same number of book-
cases.' Sabinus was none the less quite convinced that what
anyone in his household knew he knew personally. It was
Satellius, again, who started urging Sabinus, a pale and skinny
individual whose health was poor, to take up wrestling.

* Alcaeus, Sappho, Stesichorus, Ibycus, Bacchylides, Simonides,
Alcman, Anacreon, Pindar.

When Sabinus retorted: 'How can I possibly do that? It's as much as I can do to stay alive', Satellius answered: 'Now please, don't say that! Look how many slaves you've got in perfect physical condition!' A sound mind can neither be bought nor borrowed. And if it were for sale, I doubt whether it would find a buyer. And yet unsound ones are being purchased every day.

But let me pay you what I owe you and say goodbye. 'Poverty brought into accord with the law of nature is wealth.' Epicurus is constantly saying this in one way or another. But something that can never be learnt too thoroughly can never be said too often. With some people you only need to point to a remedy; others need to have it rammed into them.

LETTER XXVIII

Do you think you are the only person to have had this experience? Are you really surprised, as if it were something unprecedented, that so long a tour and such diversity of scene have not enabled you to throw off this melancholy and this feeling of depression? A change of character, not a change of air, is what you need. Though you cross the boundless ocean, though, to use the words of our poet Virgil,

> Lands and towns are left astern,*

whatever your destination you will be followed by your failings. Here is what Socrates said to someone who was making the same complaint: 'How can you wonder your travels do you no good, when you carry yourself around with you? You are saddled with the very thing that drove you away.' How can novelty of surroundings abroad and be-

* *Aeneid*, III:72.

coming acquainted with foreign scenes or cities be of any help? All that dashing about turns out to be quite futile. And if you want to know why all this running away cannot help you, the answer is simply this: you are running away in your own company. You have to lay aside the load on your spirit. Until you do that, nowhere will satisfy you. Imagine your present state as being like that of the prophetess whom our Virgil represents in a roused and excited state, largely taken over by a spirit not her own:

> The Sibyl raves about as one possessed,
> In hopes she may dislodge the mighty god
> Within her bosom.*

You rush hither and thither with the idea of dislodging a firmly seated weight when the very dashing about just adds to the trouble it causes you – like the cargo in a ship, which does not weigh her down unduly so long as it does not shift, but if it rolls more to one side than the other it is liable to carry the side on which it settles down into the water. Whatever you do is bad for you, the very movement in itself being harmful to you since you are in fact shaking up a sick man.

Once you have rid yourself of the affliction there, though, every change of scene will become a pleasure. You may be banished to the ends of the earth, and yet in whatever outlandish corner of the world you may find yourself stationed, you will find that place, whatever it may be like, a hospitable home. Where you arrive does not matter so much as what sort of person you are when you arrive there. We ought not, therefore, to give over our hearts for good to any one part of the world. We should live with the conviction: 'I wasn't born for one particular corner: the whole world's my home country.' If the truth of that were clear to you, you would not be surprised that the diversity of new surroundings for which,

* *Aeneid*, VI:78–9.

out of weariness of the old, you are constantly heading fails
to do you any good. Whichever you first came to would have
satisfied you if you had believed you were at home in all. As
it is, instead of travelling you are rambling and drifting,
exchanging one place for another when the thing you are
looking for, the good life, is available everywhere.

Could there be a scene of greater turmoil than the City? Yet
even there, if need be, you are free to lead a life of peace.
Given a free choice of posting, though, I should flee a long
way from the vicinity, let alone the sight of the City. For in
the same way as there are unpleasant climates which are
trying even to the most robust constitutions, there are others
which are none too wholesome for the mind, even though it
be a sound one, when it is still in an imperfect state and
building up its strength. I do not agree with those who
recommend a stormy life and plunge straight into the
breakers, waging a spirited struggle against wordly obstacles
every day of their lives. The wise man will put up with
these things, not go out of his way to meet them; he will
prefer a state of peace to a state of war. It does not profit a
man much to have managed to discard his own failings if he
must ever be at loggerheads with other people's. 'Socrates,'
they will tell you, 'had the Thirty Tyrants standing over him
and yet they could not break his spirit.' What difference does
it make how many masters a man has? Slavery is only one,
and yet the person who refuses to let the thought of it affect
him is a free man no matter how great the swarm of masters
around him.

It is time I left off – not before I have paid the usual duty,
though! 'A consciousness of wrongdoing is the first step to
salvation.' This remark of Epicurus' is to me a very good one.
For a person who is not aware that he is doing anything
wrong has no desire to be put right. You have to catch yourself doing it before you can reform. Some people boast about

their failings: can you imagine someone who counts his faults as merits ever giving thought to their cure? So – to the best of your ability – demonstrate your own guilt, conduct inquiries of your own into all the evidence against yourself. Play the part first of prosecutor, then of judge and finally of pleader in mitigation. Be harsh with yourself at times.

LETTER XXXIII

You feel that my present letters should be like my earlier ones and have odd sayings of leading Stoics appended to them. But they never busied themselves with philosophical gems. Their whole system is too virile for that. When things stand out and attract attention in a work you can be sure there is an uneven quality about it. One tree by itself never calls for admiration when the whole forest rises to the same height. Poetry is replete with such things; so is history. So please don't think them peculiar to Epicurus; they are general, and ours more than anyone's, although they receive more notice in him because they occur at widely scattered intervals, because they are unlooked for, and because it is rather a surprise to find spirited sayings in a person who – so most people consider – was an advocate of soft living. In my own view, Epicurus was actually, in spite of his long sleeves, a man of spirit as well. Courage, energy and a warlike spirit are as commonly given to Persians as to people with a style of dress more suited to action.

So there's no call for you to press for stock excerpts, seeing that the sort of thing which in the case of other thinkers is excerpted is in our case continuous writing. That's why we don't go in for that business of window-dressing; we don't mislead the customer, so that when he enters the shop he finds nothing in stock apart from the things on display in the window. We allow him to pick up samples from wherever he likes. And suppose we did want to separate out individual aphorisms from the mass, whom should we attribute them to? Zeno? Cleanthes? Chrysippus? Panaetius? Posidonius? We Stoics are no monarch's subjects; each asserts his own freedom. Among Epicureans whatever Hermarchus or Metrodorus says is credited to one man alone; everything ever said by any member of that fraternity was uttered under the authority and auspices of one person. I say again, then, that for us, try as we may, it is impossible to pick out individual items from so vast a stock in which each thing is as good as the next.

> The poor man 'tis that counts his flock.*

Wherever you look your eye will light on things that might stand out if everything around them were not of equal standard.

So give up this hope of being able to get an idea of the genius of the greatest figures by so cursory an approach. You have to examine and consider it as a whole. There is a sequence about the creative process, and a work of genius is a synthesis of its individual features from which nothing can be subtracted without disaster. I have no objection to your inspecting the components individually provided you do so without detaching them from the personality they actually belong to; a woman is not beautiful when her ankle or arm wins compliments, but when her total appearance diverts admiration from the individual parts of her body.

Still, if you press me I won't treat you so meanly – openhanded generosity it shall be. There is a mass of such things, an enormous mass of them, lying all over the place, needing only to be picked up as distinct from gathered up. They come,

* Ovid, *Metamorphoses*, XIII: 824.

not in dribs and drabs, but in a closely interconnected and continuous stream. I have no doubt, too, they may be very helpful to the uninitiated and those who are still novices, for individual aphorisms in a small compass, rounded off in units rather like lines of verse, become fixed more readily in the mind. It is for this reason that we give children proverbs and what the Greeks call *chriae** to learn by heart, a child's mind being able to take these in at a stage when anything more would be beyond its capacity. But in the case of a grown man who has made incontestable progress it is disgraceful to go hunting after gems of wisdom, and prop himself up with a minute number of the best-known sayings, and be dependent on his memory as well; it is time he was standing on his own feet. He should be delivering himself of such sayings, not memorizing them. It is disgraceful that a man who is old or in sight of old age should have a wisdom deriving solely from his notebook. 'Zeno said this.' And what have you said? 'Cleanthes said that.' What have you said? How much longer are you going to serve under others' orders? Assume authority yourself and utter something that may be handed down to posterity. Produce something from your own resources.

This is why I look on people like this as a spiritless lot – the people who are forever acting as interpreters and never as creators, always lurking in someone else's shadow. They never venture to do for themselves the things they have spent such a long time learning. They exercise their memories on things that are not their own. It is one thing, however, to remember, another to know. To remember is to safeguard something entrusted to your memory, whereas to know, by contrast, is actually to make each item your own, and not to be dependent on some original and be constantly looking to see what the master said. 'Zeno said this, Cleanthes that.' Let's have

*Apophthegms.

some difference between you and the books! How much longer are you going to be a pupil? From now on do some teaching as well. Why, after all, should I listen to what I can read for myself? 'The living voice,' it may be answered, 'counts for a great deal.' Not when it is just acting in a kind of secretarial capacity, making itself an instrument for what others have to say.

A further point, too, is that these people who never attain independence follow the views of their predecessors, first, in matters in which everyone else without exception has abandoned the older authority concerned, and secondly, in matters in which investigations are still not complete. But no new findings will ever be made if we rest content with the findings of the past. Besides, a man who follows someone else not only does not find anything, he is not even looking. 'But surely you are going to walk in your predecessors' footsteps?' Yes indeed, I shall use the old road, but if I find a shorter and easier one I shall open it up. The men who pioneered the old routes are leaders, not our masters. Truth lies open to everyone. There has yet to be a monopoly of truth. And there is plenty of it left for future generations too.

LETTER XXXVIII

YOU are quite right in urging that we should exchange letters oftener. The utmost benefit comes from talk because it steals little by little into the mind. Lectures prepared beforehand and delivered before a listening audience are more resounding but less intimate. Philosophy is good advice, and no one gives advice at the top of his voice. Such harangues, if I may call them that, may need to be resorted to now and then where a person in a state of indecision is needing a push. But when the object is not to make him want to learn but to get him learning, one must have recourse to these lower tones, which enter the mind more easily and stick in it. What is required is not a lot of words but effectual ones.

Words need to be sown like seed. No matter how tiny a seed may be, when it lands in the right sort of ground it unfolds its strength and from being minute expands and grows to a massive size. Reason does the same; to the outward eye its dimensions may be insignificant, but with activity it starts developing. Although the words spoken are few, if the mind has taken them in as it should they gather strength and shoot upwards. Yes, precepts have the same features as seeds: they are of compact dimensions and they produce impressive results – given, as I say, the right sort of mind, to grasp at and assimilate them. The mind will then respond by being in its turn creative and will produce a yield exceeding what was put into it.

LETTER XL

THANK you for writing so often. By doing so you give me a glimpse of yourself in the only way you can. I never get a letter from you without instantly feeling we're together. If pictures of absent friends are a source of pleasure to us, refreshing the memory and relieving the sense of void with a solace however insubstantial and unreal, how much more so are letters, which carry marks and signs of the absent friend that are real. For the handwriting of a friend affords us what is so delightful about seeing him again, the sense of recognition.

You say in your letter that you went and heard the philosopher Serapio when his ship put in where you are. 'His words,' you say, 'tend to be tumbled out at a tremendous

pace, pounded and driven along rather than poured out, for
they come in a volume no one voice could cope with.' I do
not approve of this in a philosopher, whose delivery – like
his life – should be well-ordered; nothing can be well-regu-
lated if it is done in a breakneck hurry. That is why in Homer
the impetuous type of eloquence which he compares to snow
that keeps on coming down without a break, is given to the
orator, while from the old man there comes a gentle eloquence that 'flowed sweeter than honey'.* You should take
the view, then, that this copious and impetuous energy in a
speaker is better suited to a hawker than to someone who
deals with a subject of serious importance and is also a teacher.

Yet I am just as much against his words coming in a trickle
as in a stream. He should not keep people's ears on the
stretch any more than he should swamp them. For the other
extreme of thinness and poverty means less attentiveness on
the part of the listener as he becomes tired of this slowness
with all its interruptions. Nonetheless what is waited for
does sink in more readily than what goes flying past; one
speaks in any event of instruction as being handed on to
those being taught, and something that escapes them is
hardly being handed on.

Language, moreover, which devotes its attention to truth
ought to be plain and unadorned. This popular style has
nothing to do with truth. Its object is to sway a mass audience,
to carry away unpractised ears by the force of its onslaught.
It never submits itself to detailed discussion, is just wafted
away. Besides, how can a thing possibly govern others when
it cannot be governed itself? And apart from all this surely
language which is directed to the healing of men's minds
needs to penetrate into one? Medicines do no good unless
they stop some length of time in one. There is, moreover, a
great deal of futility and emptiness about this style of speak-

* *Iliad*, III:222 and I:249.

83

ing, which has more noise about it than effectiveness. There are my terrors to be quieted, incitements to be quelled, illusions to be dispelled, extravagance to be checked, greed to be reprimanded: which of these things can be done in a hurry? What doctor can heal patients merely in passing? One might add, too, that there is not even any pleasure to be found in such a noisy promiscuous torrent of words. Just as with a lot of things that one would never believe possible one finds it quite enough to have seen them once proved possible, so with these performers with words, to have heard them once is more than enough. What is there in them, after all, that anyone could want to learn or imitate? What view is one likely to take of the state of a person's mind when his speech is wild and incoherent and knows no restraint?

This rapidity of utterance recalls a person running down a slope and unable to stop where he meant to, being carried on instead a lot farther than he intended, at the mercy of his body's momentum; it is out of control, and unbecoming to philosophy, which should be placing her words, not throwing them around, and moving forward step by step. 'But surely she can move on to a higher plane now and then as well?' Certainly, but it must be without prejudice to her dignity of character, and this vehement, excessive energy strips her of that. Power she should have, great power, but it should be controlled: she should be a never-failing stream, not a spate. Even in an advocate I should be loth to allow such uncontrollable speed in delivery, all in an unruly rush; how could a judge (who is not uncommonly, too, inexperienced and unqualified) be expected to keep up with it? Even on the occasions when an advocate is carried away by an ungovernable passion or a desire to display his powers, he should not increase his pace and pile on the words beyond the capacity of the ear.

You will be doing the right thing, therefore, if you do not

go to listen to people who are more concerned about the
quantity than the quality of what they say, and choose yourself – if you have to – to speak in the manner of Publius
Vinicius. When Asellius was asked how Vinicius spoke, he
described it as being 'at a slow pace'. Geminus Varius in
fact remarked, 'How you can call the man eloquent I simply
don't know – he can't string three words together.' Is there
any reason why of the two you should not choose Vinicius'
style? You can expect to be interrupted by persons with as
little taste as the one who, when Vinicius was jerking the
words out one by one, as if he were dictating rather than
speaking, exclaimed, 'I call on the speaker to speak.' The
pace of Quintus Haterius, a celebrated speaker of his day, is
something I should have a sensible man keep well clear of:
with him there was never a hesitation or a pause, only one
start and only one stop.

But I also think that certain styles are suitable in a greater
or lesser degree to different nationalities. In a Greek one will
tolerate this lack of discipline, while we have acquired the
habit of punctuating what we say, in writing as well as
speech. Our own Cicero, too, from whom Roman oratory
really sprang, was a steady goer. Roman discourse is more
given to self-examination, appraising itself and inviting
appraisal. Fabianus, who added outstanding oratory to those
more important distinctions of his, his way of life and his
learning, would discuss a subject with dispatch rather than
with haste. You might describe his oratory as being not
rapid but fluent. This I am ready to see in a philosopher, but
I do not insist on it; his delivery is not to be halting, but I
should rather have the words issued forth than flowing forth.
And a further reason I have for warning you against that
disease is the fact that you can only acquire it successfully if
you cease to feel any sense of shame. You really need to give
the skin of your face a good rub and then not listen to your-

self! For that unguarded pace will give rise to a lot of expressions of which you would otherwise be critical. You cannot, I repeat, successfully acquire it and preserve your modesty at the same time. One needs, moreover, constant daily practice for it. It requires a switch of attention, too, from subject-matter to words. And even if it does transpire that the words come readily to the tongue and are capable of reeling off it without any effort on your part, they will still need to be regulated. A way of speaking which is restrained, not bold, suits a wise man in the same way as an unassuming sort of walk does. The upshot, then, of what I have to say is this: I am telling you to be a slow-speaking person.

LETTER XLI

You are doing the finest possible thing and acting in your best interests if, as you say in your letter, you are persevering in your efforts to acquire a sound understanding. This is something it is foolish to pray for when you can win it from your own self. There is no need to raise our hands to heaven; there is no need to implore the temple warden to allow us close to the ear of some graven image, as though this increased the chances of our being heard. God is near you, is with you, is inside you. Yes, Lucilius, there resides within us a divine spirit, which guards us and watches us in the evil and the good we do. As we treat him, so will he treat us. No man, indeed, is good without God – is any one capable of rising above fortune unless he has help from God? He it is that prompts us to noble and exalted endeavours. In each and every good man

A god (what god we are uncertain) dwells.*

* Virgil, *Aeneid*, VIII: 352.

If you have ever come on a dense wood of ancient trees that have risen to an exceptional height, shutting out all sight of the sky with one thick screen of branches upon another, the loftiness of the forest, the seclusion of the spot, your sense of wonderment at finding so deep and unbroken a gloom out of doors, will persuade you of the presence of a deity. Any cave in which the rocks have been eroded deep into the mountain resting on it, its hollowing out into a cavern of impressive extent not produced by the labours of men but the result of processes of nature, will strike into your soul some kind of inkling of the divine. We venerate the sources of important streams; places where a mighty river bursts suddenly from hiding are provided with altars; hot springs are objects of worship; the darkness or unfathomable depth of pools has made their waters sacred. And if you come across a man who is never alarmed by dangers, never affected by cravings, happy in adversity, calm in the midst of storm, viewing mankind from a higher level and the gods from their own, is it not likely that a feeling will find its way into you of veneration for him? Is it not likely that you will say to yourself, 'Here is a thing which is too great, too sublime for anyone to regard it as being in the same sort of category as that puny body it inhabits.' Into that body there has descended a divine power. The soul that is elevated and well regulated, that passes through any experience as if it counted for comparatively little, that smiles at all the things we fear or pray for, is impelled by a force that comes from heaven. A thing of that soul's height cannot stand without the prop of a deity. Hence the greater part of it is situated where it descends from; in the same way as the sun's rays touch the earth but are really situated at the point from which they emanate, a soul possessed of greatness and holiness, which has been sent down into this world in order that we may gain a nearer knowledge of the divine, associates with us, certainly, but never loses contact with its source. On that source it depends; that is the direction in which its eyes turn, and the direction it strives to climb in; the manner in which it takes part in our affairs is that of a superior being.

What, then, is this soul? Something which has a lustre that is due to no quality other than its own. Could anything be more stupid than to praise a person for something that is not his? Or more crazy than admiring things which in a single moment can be transferred to another? It is not a golden bit that makes one horse superior to others. Sending a lion into the arena with his mane gilded, tired by the handling he has been given in the process of being forced to submit to this embellishment, is a very different thing from sending in a wild one with his spirit unbroken. Bold in attack, as nature meant him to be, in all his unkempt beauty, a beast whose glory it is that none can look on him without fear, he stands higher in people's eyes than the other, docile, gold-leaf coated creature.

No one should feel pride in anything that is not his own. We praise a vine if it loads its branches with fruit and bends its very props to the ground with the weight it carries: would any one prefer the famous vine that had gold grapes and leaves hanging on it? Fruitfulness is the vine's peculiar virtue. So, too, in a man praise is due only to what is his very own. Suppose he has a beautiful home and a handsome collection of servants, a lot of land under cultivation and a lot of money out at interest; not one of these things can be said to be in him – they are just things around him. Praise in him what can neither be given nor snatched away, what is peculiarly a man's.

You ask what that is? It is his spirit, and the perfection of his reason in that spirit. For man is a rational animal. Man's ideal state is realized when he has fulfilled the purpose for which he was born. And what is it that reason demands of

him? Something very easy – that he live in accordance with
his own nature. Yet this is turned into something difficult
by the madness that is universal among men; we push one
another into vices. And how can people be called back to
spiritual well-being when no one is trying to hold them back
and the crowd is urging them on?

LETTER XLVI

THE book you promised me has come. I was intending to
read it at my convenience and I opened it on arrival without
meaning to do any more than just get an idea of its contents.
The next thing I knew the book itself had charmed me into
a deeper reading of it there and then. How lucid its style is
you may gather from the fact that I found the work light
reading, although a first glance might well convey the
impression that the writer was someone like Livy or Epicurus,
its bulk being rather unlike you or me! It was so enjoyable,
though, that I found myself held and drawn on until I
ended up having read it right through to the end without a
break. All the time the sunshine was inviting me out, hunger
prompting me to eat, the weather threatening to break, but I
gulped it all down in one sitting.

It was a joy, not just a pleasure, to read it. There was so
much talent and spirit about it – I'd have said 'forcefulness',
too, if it had been written on a quieter plane now and then and
periodically raised on to a higher one; as it was there was no
such forcefulness, but instead there was a sustained evenness
of style. The writing was pure and virile – and yet not lacking
in that occasional entertaining touch, that bit of light relief
at the appropriate moment. The quality of nobility, of sub-

limity, you have; I want you to keep it, and to carry on just the way you're doing.

Your subject, also, contributed to the result – which is a reason why you should always select a fertile one, one that will engage the mind's attention and stimulate it. But I'll write and say more about the book when I've gone over it again. At the moment my judgement isn't really a sufficiently settled one – it's as if I'd heard it all rather than read it. You must let me go into it thoroughly, too. You needn't be apprehensive, you'll hear nothing but the truth. How fortunate you are in possessing nothing capable of inducing anyone to tell you a lie over a distance as great as the one that separates us – except that even in these circumstances, when all reason for it is removed, we still find habit a reason for telling lies!

LETTER XLVII

I'M glad to hear, from these people who've been visiting you, that you live on friendly terms with your slaves. It is just what one expects of an enlightened, cultivated person like yourself. 'They're slaves,' people say. No. They're human beings. 'They're slaves.' But they share the same roof as ourselves. 'They're slaves.' No, they're friends, humble friends. 'They're slaves.' Strictly speaking they're our fellow-slaves, if you once reflect that fortune has as much power over us as over them.

This is why I laugh at those people who think it degrading for a man to eat with his slave. Why do they think it degrading? Only because the most arrogant of conventions has decreed that the master of the house be surrounded at his dinner by a crowd of slaves, who have to stand around while he eats more than he can hold, loading an already distended belly in his monstrous greed until it proves incapable any longer of performing the function of a belly, at which point he expends more effort in vomiting everything up than he did in forcing it down. And all this time the poor slaves are forbidden to move their lips to speak, let alone to eat. The slightest murmur is checked with a stick; not even accidental sounds like a cough, or a sneeze, or a hiccup are let off a beating. All night long they go on standing about, dumb and hungry, paying grievously for any interruption.

The result is that slaves who cannot talk before his face talk about him behind his back. The slaves of former days, however, whose mouths were not sealed up like this, who were able to make conversation not only in the presence of their master but actually with him, were ready to bare their necks to the executioner for him, to divert on to themselves any danger that threatened him; they talked at dinner but under torture they kept their mouths shut. It is just this high-handed treatment which is responsible for the frequently heard saying, 'You've as many enemies as you've slaves.' They are not our enemies when we acquire them; we make them so.

For the moment I pass over other instances of our harsh and inhuman behaviour, the way we abuse them as if they were beasts of burden instead of human beings, the way for example, from the time we take our places on the dinner couches, one of them mops up the spittle and another stationed at the foot of the couch collects up the 'leavings' of the drunken diners. Another carves the costly game birds, slicing off choice pieces from the breast and rump with the unerring strokes of a trained hand – unhappy man, to exist for the one and only purpose of carving a fat bird in the proper style – although the person who learns the technique from sheer necessity is not quite so much to be pitied as the person who gives demonstrations of it for pleasure's sake. Another, the one who serves the wine, is got up like a girl and engaged in a struggle with his years; he cannot get away from his boyhood, but is dragged back to it all the time; although he already has the figure of a soldier, he is kept free of hair by having it rubbed away or pulled out by the roots. His sleepless night is divided between his master's drunkenness and sexual pleasures, boy at the table, man in the bedroom. Another, who has the privilege of rating each guest's character, has to go on standing where he is, poor fellow, and watch to see whose powers of flattery and absence of restraint in appetite or speech are to secure them an invitation for the following day. Add to these the caterers with their highly developed knowledge of their master's palate, the men who know the flavours that will sharpen his appetite, know what will appeal to his eyes, what novelties can tempt his stomach when it is becoming queasy, what dishes he will push aside with the eventual coming of sheer satiety, what he will have a craving for on that particular day.

These are the people with whom a master cannot tolerate the thought of taking his dinner, assuming that to sit down at the same table with one of his slaves would seriously impair his dignity. 'The very idea!' he says. Yet have a look at the number of masters he has from the ranks of these very slaves.* Take Callistus' one-time master. I saw him once actually standing waiting at Callistus' door and refused admission while others were going inside, the very master who had attached a price-ticket to the man and put him up for sale along with other rejects from his household staff. There's a slave who has paid his master back – one who was pushed into the first lot, too, the batch on which the auctioneer is merely trying out his voice! Now it was the slave's turn to strike his master off his list, to decide that *he*'s not the sort of

* Many ex-slaves had risen to high positions under Claudius and Nero.

person he wants in *his* house. Callistus' master sold him, yes, and look how much it cost him!

How about reflecting that the person you call your slave traces his origin back to the same stock as yourself, has the same good sky above him, breathes as you do, lives as you do, dies as you do? It is as easy for you to see in him a free-born man as for him to see a slave in you. Remember the Varus disaster: many a man of the most distinguished ancestry, who was doing his military service as the first step on the road to a seat in the Senate, was brought low by fortune, condemned by her to look after a steading, for example, or a flock of sheep. Now think contemptuously of these people's lot in life, in whose very place, for all your contempt, you could suddenly find yourself.

I don't want to involve myself in an endless topic of debate by discussing the treatment of slaves, towards whom we Romans are exceptionally arrogant, harsh and insulting. But the essence of the advice I'd like to give is this: treat your inferiors in the way in which you would like to be treated by your own superiors. And whenever it strikes you how much power you have over your slave, let it also strike you that your own master has just as much power over you. 'I haven't got a master,' you say. You're young yet; there's always the chance that you'll have one. Have you forgotten the age at which Hecuba became a slave, or Croesus, or the mother of Darius, or Plato, or Diogenes? Be kind and courteous in your dealings with a slave; bring him into your discussions and conversations and your company generally. And if at this point all those people who have been spoilt by luxury raise an outcry protesting, as they will, 'There couldn't be anything more degrading, anything more disgraceful', let me just say that these are the very persons I will catch on occasion kissing the hand of someone else's slave.

Don't you notice, too, how our ancestors took away all

odium from the master's position and all that seemed insulting or degrading in the lot of the slave by calling the master 'father of the household' and speaking of the slaves as 'members of the household' (something which survives to this day in the mime)? They instituted, too, a holiday on which master and slave were to eat together, not as the only day this could happen, of course, but as one on which it was always to happen. And in the household they allowed the slaves to hold official positions and to exercise some jurisdiction in it; in fact they regarded the household as a miniature republic.

'Do you mean to say,' comes the retort, 'that I'm to have each and every one of my slaves sitting at the table with me?' Not at all, any more than you're to invite to it everybody who isn't a slave. You're quite mistaken, though, if you imagine that I'd bar from the table certain slaves on the grounds of the relatively menial or dirty nature of their work – that muleteer, for example, or that cowhand. I propose to value them according to their character, not their jobs. Each man has a character of his own choosing; it is chance or fate that decides his choice of job. Have some of them dine with you because they deserve it, others in order to make them so deserving. For if there's anything typical of the slave about them as a result of the low company they're used to living in, it will be rubbed off through association with men of better breeding.

You needn't, my dear Lucilius, look for friends only in the City or the Senate; if you keep your eyes open, you'll find them in your own home. Good material often lies idle for want of someone to make use of it; just give it a trial. A man who examines the saddle and bridle and not the animal itself when he is out to buy a horse is a fool; similarly, only an absolute fool values a man according to his clothes, or according to his social position, which after all is only something that we wear like clothing.

'He's a slave.' But he may have the spirit of a free man. 'He's a slave.' But is that really to count against him? Show me a man who isn't a slave; one is a slave to sex, another to money, another to ambition; all are slaves to hope or fear. I could show you a man who has been a Consul who is a slave to his 'little old woman', a millionaire who is the slave of a little girl in domestic service. I could show you some highly aristocratic young men who are utter slaves to stage artistes. And there's no state of slavery more disgraceful than one which is self-imposed. So you needn't allow yourself to be deterred by the snobbish people I've been talking about from showing good humour towards your slaves instead of adopting an attitude of arrogant superiority towards them. Have them respect you rather than fear you.

Here, just because I've said they 'should respect a master rather than fear him', someone will tell us that I'm now inviting slaves to proclaim their freedom and bringing about their employers' overthrow. 'Are slaves to pay their "respects" like dependent followers or early morning callers? That's what he means, I suppose.' Anyone saying this forgets that what is enough for a god, in the shape of worship, cannot be too little for a master. To be really respected is to be loved; and love and fear will not mix. That's why I think you're absolutely right in not wishing to be feared by your slaves, and in confining your lashings to verbal ones; as instruments of correction, beatings are for animals only. Besides, what annoys us does not necessarily do us any harm; but we masters are apt to be robbed of our senses by mere passing fancies, to the point where our anger is called out by anything which fails to answer to our will. We assume the mental attitudes of tyrants. For they too forget their own strength and the help-lessness of others and grow white-hot with fury as if they had received an injury, when all the time they are quite immune from any such danger through the sheer exaltedness of their position. Nor indeed are they unaware of this; but it does not stop them seizing an opportunity of finding fault with an inferior and maltreating him for it; they receive an injury by way of excuse to do one themselves.

But I won't keep you any longer; you don't need exhortation. It is a mark of a good way of life that, among other things, it satisfies and abides; bad behaviour, constantly changing, not for the better, simply into different forms, has none of this stability.

LETTER XLVIII

I SHALL reply later to the letter you sent me while you were on your journey – it was as long as the journey itself! I must first take myself aside and deliberate what advice I should give. For you yourself, before consulting me as you are doing, gave long thought to the question whether you should consult me at all, so I ought to be giving this question of advice far longer thought, on the principle that it takes you more time to solve a problem than to set it. Particularly when one course is to your interest and another to mine – or does this make me sound like an Epicurean again? No, if a thing is in your interest it is also in my own interest. Otherwise, if any matter that affects you is no concern of mine, I am not a friend. Friendship creates a community of interest between us in everything. We have neither successes nor setbacks as individuals; our lives have a common end. No one can lead a happy life if he thinks only of himself and turns everything to his own purposes. You should live for the other person if you wish to live for yourself. The assiduous and scrupulous cultivation of this bond, which leads to our associating with our fellow-men and believes in the existence of a common law for all mankind, contributes more than anything else to the maintenance of that more intimate bond I was mentioning, friendship. A person who shares much with a fellow human being will share everything with a friend.

What I should like those subtle thinkers – you know the ones I mean, my peerless Lucilius – to teach me is this, what my duties are to a friend and to a man, rather than the number of senses in which the expression 'friend' is used and how many different meanings the word 'man' has. Before my very eyes wisdom and folly are taking their separate stands: which shall I join, whose side am I to follow? For one person 'man' is equivalent to 'friend', for another 'man' and 'friend' are far from being identified, and in making a friend one man will be seeking an asset while another will be making himself an asset to the other; and in the midst of all this what you people do for me is pull words about and cut up syllables. One is led to believe that unless one has constructed syllogisms of the craftiest kind, and reduced fallacies to a compact form in which a false conclusion is derived from a true premise, one will not be in a position to distinguish what one should aim at and what one should avoid. It makes one ashamed – that men of our advanced years should turn a thing as serious as this into a game.

'Mouse is a syllable, and a mouse nibbles cheese; therefore, a syllable nibbles cheese.' Suppose for the moment I can't detect the fallacy in that. What danger am I placed in by such lack of insight? What serious consequences are there in it for me? What I have to fear, no doubt, is the possibility, one of these days, of my catching a syllable in a mousetrap or even having my cheese eaten up by a book if I'm not careful. Unless perhaps the following train of logic is a more acute one: 'Mouse is a syllable, and a syllable does not nibble cheese; therefore, a mouse does not nibble cheese.' What childish fatuities these are! Is this what we philosophers acquire wrinkles in our brows for? Is this what we let our beards grow long for? Is this what we teach with faces grave and pale?

Shall I tell you what philosophy holds out to humanity? Counsel. One person is facing death, another is vexed by poverty, while another is tormented by wealth – whether his own or someone else's; one man is appalled by his misfortunes while another longs to get away from his own prosperity; one man is suffering at the hands of men, another at the hands of the gods. What's the point of concocting whimsies for me of the sort I've just been mentioning? This isn't the place for fun – you're called in to help the unhappy. You're pledged to bring succour to the shipwrecked, to those in captivity, to the sick, the needy and men who are just placing their heads beneath the executioner's uplifted axe. Where are you off to? What are you about? The person you're engaging in word-play with is in fear – go to his aid. . . .*
All mankind are stretching out their hands to you on every side. Lives that have been ruined, lives that are on the way to ruin are appealing for some help; it is to you that they look for hope and assistance. They are begging you to extricate them from this awful vortex, to show them in their doubt and disarray the shining torch of truth. Tell them what nature has made necessary and what she has made superfluous. Tell them how simple are the laws she has laid down, and how straightforward and enjoyable life is for those who follow them and how confused and disagreeable it is for others who put more trust in popular ideas than they do in nature. All right if you can point out to me where those puzzles are likely to bring such people relief. Which of them removes cravings or brings them under control? If only they were simply

* The text for three or four words is corrupt to the point of being untranslatable.

unhelpful! They're actually harmful. I'll give you the clearest proof whenever you like of their tendency to weaken and enfeeble even eminent talents once applied to such quibbles. And when it comes to saying how they equip people proposing to do battle with fortune and what weapons they offer them, one hangs one's head with shame. Is this the way to our supreme ideal? Do we get there by means of all that 'if X, Y, or if not Y, Z' one finds in philosophy? And by means of quibbles that would be shameful and discreditable even among persons occupying themselves with law reports? When you're leading the person you're questioning into a trap, aren't you just making it look as if he has lost his case on a purely technical point of pleading? The praetor's court, however, restores litigants losing in this way to their rightful position, and philosophy does the same for the people thus questioned. Why do philosophers like you abandon the magnificent promises you have made? After assuring me in solemn terms that you will see to it that my eyes shall no more be overwhelmed by the glitter of gold than by the glitter of a sword, that I shall spurn with magnificent strength of purpose the things all other men pray for and the things all other men are afraid of, why do you have to descend to the schoolroom A B C? What do you say?

Is this the way to the heavens?*

For that is what philosophy has promised me – that she will make me God's equal. That's the invitation and that's what I've come for; be as good as your word.

Keep clear, then, my dear Lucilius, as far as you can, of the sort of quibbles and qualifications I've been mentioning in philosophers. Straightforwardness and simplicity are in keeping with goodness. Even if you had a large part of your

* *Sic itur ad astra?* Virgil, *Aeneid*, IX:641.

life remaining before you, you would have to organize it very economically to have enough for all the things that are necessary; as things are, isn't it the height of folly to learn inessential things when time's so desperately short!

LETTER LIII

I WONDER whether there's anything I couldn't be persuaded into now, after letting myself be persuaded recently into taking a trip by sea. The sea was quite calm when we cast off. The sky was certainly heavily overcast, with the kind of dark clouds that generally break in a squall or downpour. But in spite of the uncertain, threatening skies, I thought it would be perfectly feasible to make it across the few miles from your Parthenope over to Puteoli. And so, with the object of getting the crossing over quicker, I headed straight for Nesis over the open water to cut out all the intervening curves of the coast-line. Now when I had got so far across that it made no odds whether I went on or turned back, first of all the smoothness which had tempted me to my undoing disappeared. There was no storm as yet, but a heavy swell was running by then and the waves were steadily getting rougher. I began asking the helmsman to put me ashore somewhere. He kept saying the coast was a rugged one without a haven anywhere and that there was nothing he feared quite so much in a storm as a lee shore. I was in far too bad a way, though, for any thought of possible danger to enter my head, as I was suffering the torments of that sluggish brand of seasickness that will not bring one relief, the kind that upsets the stomach without clearing it. So I put pressure on him and compelled him, willy-nilly, to make for the shore. Once we

were close in there was no waiting on my part for anything
to be done in the manner commended by Virgil,

> Bows faced seawards

or

> Anchor cast from bow.*

Remembering my training as a long-standing devotee of
cold baths, I dived into the sea in just the way a cold-water
addict ought to – in my woolly clothes. You can imagine
what I suffered as I crawled out over the rocks, as I searched
for a route to safety or fought my way there. It made me
realize how right sailors are in being afraid of a lee shore.
What I endured, in my inability to endure my then self, is
beyond belief. You can take it from me that the reason
Ulysses got himself wrecked everywhere was not so much
because Neptune was against him from the day he was born,
but because he was given to seasickness like me – it'll take *me*
twenty years to reach my destination, too, if I ever have to
journey anywhere by sea!

As soon as I'd settled my stomach (for stomachs, as you
know, aren't clear of seasickness the moment they're clear of
the sea) and rubbed myself over with embrocation to put
some life back into my body, I began to reflect how we are
attended by an appalling forgetfulness of our weaknesses,
even the physical ones which are continually bringing themselves to our notice, and much more so with those that are
not only more serious but correspondingly less apparent. A
slight feverishness may deceive a person, but when it has
developed to the point where a genuine fever is raging it will
extract an admission that something is wrong from even a
tough and hardened individual. Suppose our feet ache, with
little needling pains in the joints: at this stage we pass it off
and say we've sprained an ankle or strained something in

* *Aeneid*, VI:3, III:277.

some exercise or other; while the disorder is in its indeterminate, commencing phase, its name eludes us, but once it starts bending the feet in just the way an ankle-rack does and makes them both misshapen, we have to confess that we've got the gout.

With afflictions of the spirit, though, the opposite is the case: the worse a person is, the less he feels it. You needn't feel surprised, my dearest Lucilius; a person sleeping lightly perceives impressions in his dreams and is sometimes, even, aware during sleep that he is asleep, whereas a heavy slumber blots out even dreams and plunges the mind too deep for consciousness of self. Why does no one admit his failings? Because he's still deep in them. It's the person who's awakened who recounts his dream, and acknowledging one's failings is a sign of health. So let us rouse ourselves, so that we may be able to demonstrate our errors. But only philosophy will wake us; only philosophy will shake us out of that heavy sleep. Devote yourself entirely to her. You're worthy of her, she's worthy of you – fall into each other's arms. Say a firm, plain no to every other occupation. There's no excuse for your pursuing philosophy merely in moments when occasion allows. If you were sick you would take a rest from attending to your personal affairs and drop your practice in the courts. And during a spell of improvement in your condition you wouldn't look on any client as being so important that you'd undertake his case in court. No, you'd devote your entire attention to recovering from your illness in the quickest possible time. Well, then, aren't you going to do the same in these circumstances? Away with every obstacle and leave yourself free to acquire a sound mind – no one ever attains this if he's busy with other things. Philosophy wields an authority of her own; she doesn't just accept time, she grants one it. She's not something one takes up in odd moments. She's an active, full-time mistress, ever present and demand-

ing. When some state or other offered Alexander a part of
its territory and half of all its property he told them that 'he
hadn't come to Asia with the intention of accepting whatever
they cared to give him, but of letting them keep whatever
he chose to leave them.' Philosophy, likewise, tells all other
occupations: 'It's not my intention to accept whatever time
is left over from you; you shall have, instead, what I reject.'

Give your whole mind to her. Sit at her side and pay her
constant court, and an enormous gap will widen between
yourself and other men. You'll end up far in advance of all
mankind, and not far behind the gods themselves. Would
you like to know what the actual difference between yourself
and the gods will be? They will exist for longer. And yet
to me what an indisputable mark it is of a great artist to have
captured everything in a tiny compass; a wise man has as
much scope before him as a god with all eternity in front of
him. There is one thing, too, in which the wise man actually
surpasses any god: a god has nature to thank for his immunity
from fear, while the wise man can thank his own efforts for
this. Look at that for an achievement, to have all the frailty
of a human being and all the freedom from care of a god.
Philosophy's power to blunt all the blows of circumstance is
beyond belief. Never a missile lodges in her; she has strong,
impenetrable defences; some blows she breaks the force of,
parrying them with the slack of her gown as if they were
trivial, others she flings off and hurls back at the sender.

LETTER LIV

ILL health – which had granted me quite a long spell of
leave – has attacked me without warning again. 'What kind
of ill health?' you'll be asking. And well you may, for there

isn't a single kind I haven't experienced. There's one particular ailment, though, for which I've always been singled out, so to speak. I see no reason why I should call it by its Greek name,* difficulty in breathing being a perfectly good way of describing it. Its onslaught is of very brief duration – like a squall, it is generally over within the hour. One could hardly, after all, expect anyone to keep on drawing his last breath for long, could one? I've been visited by all the troublesome or dangerous complaints there are, and none of them, in my opinion, is more unpleasant than this one – which is hardly surprising, is it, when you consider that with anything else you're merely ill, while with this you're constantly at your last gasp? This is why doctors have nicknamed it 'rehearsing death', since sooner or later the breath does just what it has been trying to do all those times. Do you imagine that as I write this I must be feeling in high spirits at having escaped this time? No, it would be just as absurd for me to feel over-joyed at its being over – as if this meant I was a healthy man again – as it would be for a person to think he has won his case on obtaining an extension of time before trial.

Even as I fought for breath, though, I never ceased to find comfort in cheerful and courageous reflections. 'What's this?' I said. 'So death is having all these tries at me, is he? Let him, then! I had a try at him a long while ago myself.' 'When was this?' you'll say. Before I was born. Death is just not being. What that is like I know already. It will be the same after me as it was before me. If there is any torment in the later state, there must also have been torment in the period before we saw the light of day; yet we never felt conscious of any distress then. I ask you, wouldn't you say that anyone who took the view that a lamp was worse off when it was put out than it was before it was lit was an utter idiot? We, too, are lit and put out. We suffer somewhat in the intervening period, but

* i.e. its medical name, *asthma*.

at either end of it there is a deep tranquillity. For, unless I'm mistaken, we are wrong, my dear Lucilius, in holding that death follows after, when in fact it precedes as well as succeeds. Death is all that was before us. What does it matter, after all, whether you cease to be or never begin, when the result of either is that you do not exist?

I kept on talking to myself in these and similar terms – silently, needless to say, words being out of the question. Then little by little the affliction in my breathing, which was coming to be little more than a panting now, came on at longer intervals and slackened away. It has lasted on, all the same, and in spite of the passing of this attack, my breathing is not yet coming naturally. I feel a sort of catch and hesitation in it. Let it do as it pleases, though, so long as the sighs aren't heartfelt. You can feel assured on my score of this: I shall not be afraid when the last hour comes – I'm already prepared, not planning as much as a day ahead. The man, though, whom you should admire and imitate is the one who finds it a joy to live and in spite of that is not reluctant to die. For where's the virtue in going out when you're really being thrown out? And yet there is this virtue about my case: I'm in the process of being thrown out, certainly, but the manner of it is as if I were going out. And the reason why it never happens to a wise man is that being thrown out signifies expulsion from a place one is reluctant to depart from, and there is nothing the wise man does reluctantly. He escapes necessity because he wills what necessity is going to force on him.

LETTER LV

I'VE just this moment returned from a ride in my sedan-chair, feeling as tired as if I'd walked the whole distance instead of being seated all the way. Even to be carried for any length of time is hard work, and all the more so, I dare say, because it is unnatural, nature having given us legs with which to do our own walking, just as she gave us eyes with which to do our own seeing. Soft living imposes on us the penalty of debility; we cease to be able to do the things we've long been grudging about doing. However, I was needing to give my body a shaking up, either to dislodge some phlegm, perhaps, that had collected in my throat, or to have some thickness, due to one cause or another, in my actual breathing reduced by the motion, which I've noticed before has done me some good. So I deliberately continued the ride for quite a long way, with the beach itself tempting me onwards. It sweeps round between Cumae and Servilius Vatia's country house in a sort of narrow causeway with the sea on one side and a lagoon on the other. A recent storm had left it firm; for, as you know, a fast-running heavy surf makes a beach flat and smooth, while a longish period of calm weather leads to a disintegration of this surface with the disappearance of the moisture that binds the particles of sand together.

I had started looking around me in my usual way to see whether I could find anything I could turn to good account, when my eyes turned to the house which had once belonged to Vatia. This was the place where Vatia passed the latter part of his life, a wealthy man who had held the office of praetor but was famed for nothing but his life of retirement, and considered a fortunate man on that ground alone. For whenever a man was ruined through being a friend of Asinius Gallus or an enemy of Sejanus, or devoted to Sejanus (for it came to be as dangerous to have been a follower of his as it was to cross him), people used to exclaim, 'Vatia, you're the only person who knows how to live!' What in fact he knew was how to hide rather than how to live. And there is a lot of difference between your life being a retiring one and its being a spineless one. I never used to pass this house while Vatia was alive without saying, 'Here lieth Vatia.' But philosophy, my dear Lucilius, is such a holy thing and inspires so much respect, that even something that resembles it has a specious appeal. Let a man retire and the common crowd will think of him as leading a life apart, free of all cares, self-contented, living for himself, when in fact not one of these blessings can be won by anyone other than the philosopher. He alone knows how to live for himself: he is the one, in fact, who knows the fundamental thing, how to live. The person who has run away from the world and his fellow-men, whose exile is due to the unsuccessful outcome of his own desires, who is unable to endure the sight of others more fortunate, who has taken to some place of hiding in his alarm like a timid, inert animal, he is not 'living for himself', but for his belly and his sleep and his passions – in utter degradation, in other words. The fact that a person is living for nobody does not automatically mean that he is living for himself. Still, a persevering steadfastness of purpose counts for a lot, so that even inertia if stubbornly maintained may carry a certain weight.

I can't give you any accurate information about the house itself. I only know the front of it and the parts in view, the parts that it displays even to passers-by. There are two artificial grottoes, considerable feats of engineering, each as big as the most spacious hall, one of them not letting in the sun at all, the other retaining it right up until its setting. There is a grove of plane trees through the middle of which runs a stream flowing alternately, like a tide-race, into the sea and into the Acherusian Lake, a stream capable of supporting a stock of fish even if constantly exploited; it is left alone, though, when the sea is open: only when bad weather gives the fishermen a holiday do they lay hands on this ready supply. But the most advantageous feature of the house is that it has Baiae next door; it enjoys all the amenities of that resort and is free from its disadvantages. I can speak for these attractions from personal knowledge, and I am quite prepared to believe, too, that it is an all-the-year-round house, since it lies in the path of the western breeze, catching it to such an extent as to exclude Baiae from the benefit of it. Vatia seems to have been no fool in choosing this place as the one in which he would spend his retirement, sluggish and senile as that retirement had become.

The place one's in, though, doesn't make any contribution to peace of mind: it's the spirit that makes everything agreeable to oneself. I've seen for myself people sunk in gloom in cheerful and delightful country houses, and people in completely secluded surroundings who looked as if they were run off their feet. So there's no reason why you should feel that you're not as much at rest in your mind as you might be just because you're not here in Campania. Why aren't you, for that matter? Transmit your thoughts all the way here. There's nothing to stop you enjoying the company of absent friends, as often as you like, too, and for as long as you like. This pleasure in their company – and there's no greater pleasure – is one we enjoy the more when we're absent from one another. For having our friends present makes us spoilt; as a result of our talking and walking and sitting together every now and then, on being separated we haven't a thought for those we've just been seeing. One good reason, too, why we should endure the absence patiently is the fact that every one of us is absent to a great extent from his friends even when they are around. Count up in this connexion first the nights spent away from one another, then the different engagements that keep each one busy, then the time passed in the privacy of one's study and in trips into the country, and you'll see that periods abroad don't deprive us of so very much. Possession of a friend should be with the spirit: the spirit's never absent: it sees daily whoever it likes. So share with me my studies, my meals, my walks. Life would be restricted indeed if there were any barrier to our imaginations. I see you, my dear Lucilius, I hear you at this very moment. I feel so very much with you that I wonder whether I shouldn't start writing you notes rather than letters!

LETTER LVI

I CANNOT for the life of me see that quiet is as necessary to a person who has shut himself away to do some studying as it is usually thought to be. Picture me with a babel of noise going on all about me, staying right over a public bath-house. Now imagine to yourself all manner of sounds that can get you hating your ears. When the strenuous types are doing their exercises, swinging weight-laden hands about, I hear the grunting as they toil away – or go through the motions of toiling away – at them, and the hissings and strident gasps every time they expel their pent up breath. When my attention turns to a less active fellow who is contenting himself with an ordinary inexpensive massage, I hear the smack of a hand pummelling his shoulders, the sound varying according as it comes down flat or cupped. But if on top of this some ball player comes along and starts shouting out the score, one's done for! Now add someone starting up a brawl, and someone else caught thieving, and the fellow who likes the sound of his voice in the bath, and the people who leap into the pool with a tremendous splash. Going beyond those sounds which are straightforward if nothing else, call to mind the hair remover, repeatedly giving vent to his shrill and penetrating cry the better to advertise his presence, never silent unless it be while he is plucking someone's armpits and making the client yell for him! Then think of the various cries of the

man selling drinks, and the one selling sausages and the other
selling pastries, and all the ones hawking for the catering shops,
each publicizing his wares with a distinctive cry of his own.

'You must be made of iron,' you may say, 'or else hard of
hearing if your mind is unaffected by all this babel of dis-
cordant noises around you, when continual "good morning"
greetings were enough to finish off the Stoic Chrysippus!'
But I swear I no more notice all this roar of noise than I do
the sound of waves or falling water – even if I am here told
the story of a people on the Nile who moved their capital
solely because they could not stand the thundering of a
cataract! Voices, I think, are more inclined to distract one
than general noise; noise merely fills one's ears, battering
away at them while voices actually catch one's attention.
Among the things which create a racket all around me without
distracting me at all I include the carriages hurrying by in the
street, the carpenter who works in the same block, a man in
the neighbourhood who saws, and this fellow tuning horns
and flutes at the Trickling Fountain and emitting blasts instead of music. I still find an intermittent noise more irritating
than a continuous one. But by now I have so steeled myself
against all these things that I can even put up with a coxswain's
strident tones as he gives his oarsmen the rhythm. For I
force my mind to become self-absorbed and not let outside
things distract it. There can be absolute bedlam without so
long as there is no commotion within, so long as fear and
desire are not at loggerheads, so long as meanness and extravagance are not at odds and harassing each other. For what
is the good of having silence throughout the neighbourhood
if one's emotions are in turmoil?

> The peaceful stillness of the night had lulled
> The world to rest.*

* A fragment of Varro Atacinus' translation from the Greek of
Apollonius' *Argonautica*.

This is incorrect. There is no such thing as 'peaceful stillness' except where reason has lulled it to rest. Night does not remove our worries; it brings them to the surface. All it gives us is a change of anxieties. For even when people are asleep they have dreams as troubled as their days. The only true serenity is the one which represents the free development of a sound mind. Look at the man whose quest for sleep demands absolute quiet from his spacious house. To prevent any sound disturbing his ears every one of his host of slaves preserves total silence and those who come anywhere near him walk on tip-toe. Naturally enough he tosses from side to side, trying to snatch some fitful sleep in between the spells of fretting, and complains of having heard sounds when he never heard them at all. And what do you suppose is the reason? His mind is in a ferment. It is this which needs to be set at peace. Here is the mutiny that needs to be suppressed. The fact that the body is lying down is no reason for supposing that the mind is at peace. Rest is sometimes far from restful. Hence our need to be stimulated into general activity and kept occupied and busy with pursuits of the right nature whenever we are victims of the sort of idleness that wearies of itself. When great military commanders notice indiscipline among their men they suppress it by giving them some work to do, mounting expeditions to keep them actively employed. People who are really busy never have enough time to become skittish. And there is nothing so certain as the fact that the harmful consequences of inactivity are dissipated by activity.

We commonly give the impression that the reasons for our having gone into political retirement are our disgust with public life and our dissatisfaction with some uncongenial and unrewarding post. Yet every now and then ambition rears its head again in the retreat into which we were really driven by our apprehensions and our waning interest; for our ambition did not cease because it had been rooted out, but merely because it had tired – or become piqued, perhaps, at its lack of success. I would say the same about extravagant living, which appears on occasion to have left one and then, when one has declared for the simple life, places temptation in the way. In the middle of one's programme of frugality it sets out after pleasures which one had discarded but not condemned, its pursuit of them indeed being all the more ardent the less one is aware of it. For when they are in the open vices invariably take a more moderate form; diseases too are on the way towards being cured when once they have broken out, instead of being latent, and made their presence felt. So it is with the love of money, the love of power and the other maladies that affect the minds of men – you may be sure that it is when they abate and give every appearance of being cured that they are at their most dangerous. We give the impression of being in retirement, and are nothing of the kind. For if we are genuine in this, if we have sounded the retreat and really turned away from the surface show, then, as I was saying a little while ago, nothing will distract us. Men and birds together in full chorus will never break into our thinking when that thinking is good and has at last come to be of a sure and steady character.

The temperament that starts at the sound of a voice or chance noises in general is an unstable one and one that has yet to attain inward detachment. It has an element of uneasiness in it, and an element of the rooted fear that makes a man a prey to anxiety, as in the description given by our Virgil:

> And I, who formerly would never flinch
> At flying spears or serried ranks of Greeks,
> Am now alarmed by every breeze and roused
> By every sound to nervousness, in fear
> For this companion and this load alike.*

* *Aeneid*, II:726–9. Aeneas is describing his feelings as he leads his son and carries his father out of Troy while the city is being sacked.

The earlier character here is the wise man, who knows no fear at the hurtling of missiles, or the clash of weapons against weapons in the close-packed ranks, or the thunderous noise of a city in destruction. The other, later one has everything to learn; fearing for his belongings he pales at every noise; a single cry, whatever it is, prostrates him, being immediately taken for the yelling of the enemy; the slightest movement frightens him out of his life; his baggage makes him a coward. Pick out any one of your 'successful' men, with all they trail or carry about with them, and you will have a picture of the man 'in fear for this companion and this load'. You may be sure, then, that you are at last 'lulled to rest' when noise never reaches you and when voices never shake you out of yourself, whether they be menacing or inviting or just a meaningless hubbub of empty sound all round you.

'This is all very well,' you may say, 'but isn't it sometimes a lot simpler just to keep away from the din?' I concede that, and in fact it is the reason why I shall shortly be moving elsewhere. What I wanted was to give myself a test and some practice. Why should I need to suffer the torture any longer than I want to when Ulysses found so easy a remedy for his companions even against the Sirens?*

LETTER LXIII

I AM very sorry to hear of your friend Flaccus' death. Still, I would not have you grieve unduly over it. I can scarcely venture to demand that you should not grieve at all – and yet I am convinced that it is better that way. But who will ever

* Homer narrates in Book XII of the Odyssey how the hero, following the advice of Circe, stopped the ears of his crew with beeswax while they rowed past the place where the temptresses sang.

be granted that strength of character, unless he be a man already lifted far out of fortune's reach? Even he will feel a twinge of pain when a thing like this happens – but only a twinge. As for us, we can be pardoned for having given way to tears so long as they have not run down in excessive quantities and we have checked them for ourselves. When one has lost a friend one's eyes should be neither dry nor streaming. Tears, yes, there should be, but not lamentation. Can you find the rule I am laying down a harsh one when the greatest of Greek poets has restricted to a single day, no more, a person's right to cry – in the passage where he tells us that even Niobe remembered to eat?* Would you like to know what lies behind extravagant weeping and wailing? In our tears we are trying to find means of proving that we feel the loss. We are not being governed by our grief but parading it. No one ever goes into mourning for the benefit merely of himself. Oh, the miserable folly of it all – that there should be an element of ostentation in grief!

'Come now,' you will be asking, 'are you saying that I should forget a person who has been a friend?' Well, you are not proposing to keep him very long in your memory if his memory is to last just as long as your grief. At any moment something or other will happen that will turn that long face of yours into a smiling one. I do not see very much time going by before the sense of loss is mitigated and even the keenest sorrowings settle down. Your face will cease to be its present picture of sadness as soon as you take your eyes off yourself. At the moment you are keeping a watch on your grief – but even as you do it is fading away, and the keener it is the quicker it is in stopping.

Let us see to it that the recollection of those we have lost becomes a pleasure to us. Nobody really cares to cast his mind back to something which he is never going to think of

* Homer, *Iliad*, XIX:228f., XXIV:601f.

without pain. Inevitable as it is that the names of persons who were dear to us and are now lost should cause us a gnawing sort of pain when we think of them, that pain is not without a pleasure of its own. As my teacher Attalus used to say, 'In the pleasure we find in the memory of departed friends there is a resemblance to the way in which certain bitter fruits are agreeable or the very acidity of an exceedingly old wine has its attraction. But after a certain interval all that pained us is obliterated and the enjoyment comes to us unalloyed.' If we are to believe him, 'Thinking of friends who are alive and well is like feasting on cakes and honey. Recalling those who are gone is pleasant but not without a touch of sourness. Who would deny, though, that even acid things like this with a harshness in their taste do stimulate the palate?' Personally I do not agree with him there. Thinking of departed friends is to me something sweet and mellow. For when I had them with me it was with the feeling that I was going to lose them, and now that I have lost them I keep the feeling that I have them with me still.

So, my dear Lucilius, behave in keeping with your usual fair-mindedness and stop misinterpreting the kindness of fortune. She has given as well as taken away. Let us therefore go all out to make the most of friends, since no one can tell how long we shall have the opportunity. Let us just think how often we leave them behind when we are setting out on some long journey or other, or how often we fail to see them when we are staying in the same area, and we shall realize that we have lost all too much time while they are still alive. Can you stand people who treat their friends with complete neglect and then mourn them to distraction, never caring about anyone unless they have lost him? And the reason they lament them so extravagantly then is that they are afraid people may wonder whether they did care; they are looking for belated means of demonstrating their devotion. If we have

other friends, we are hardly kind or appreciative of them if
they count for so very little when it comes to consoling us
for the one we have buried. If we have no other friends, we
have done ourselves a greater injury than fortune has done us:
she has deprived us of a single friend but we have deprived
ourselves of every friend we have failed to make. A person,
moreover, who has not been able to care about more than
one friend cannot have cared even about that one too much.
Supposing someone lost his one and only shirt in a robbery,
would you not think him an utter idiot if he chose to bewail
his loss rather than look about him for some means of keeping out the cold and find something to put over his shoulders?
You have buried someone you loved. Now look for someone
to love. It is better to make good the loss of a friend than to
cry over him.

What I am about to go on to say is, I know, a commonplace, but I am not going to omit it merely because every one
has said it. Even a person who has not deliberately put an
end to his grief finds an end to it in the passing of time. And
merely growing weary of sorrowing is quite shameful as a
means of curing sorrow in the case of an enlightened man. I
should prefer to see you abandoning grief than it abandoning
you. Much as you may wish to, you will not be able to keep it
up for very long, so give it up as early as possible. For women
our forefathers fixed the period of mourning at a year with
the intention, not that women should continue mourning as
long as that, but that they should not go on any longer: for
men no period is prescribed at all because none would be
decent. Yet out of all the pathetic females you know of who
were only dragged away from the graveside, or even torn
from the body itself, with the greatest of difficulty, can you
show me one whose tears lasted for a whole month? Nothing
makes itself unpopular quite so quickly as a person's grief.
When it is fresh it attracts people to its side, finds someone to

offer it consolation; but if it is perpetuated it becomes an object of ridicule – deservedly, too, for it is either feigned or foolish.

And all this comes to you from me, the very man who wept for Annaeus Serenus, that dearest of friends to me, so unrestrainedly that I must needs be included – though this is the last thing I should want – among examples of men who have been defeated by grief! Nevertheless I condemn today the way I behaved then. I realize now that my sorrowing in the way I did was mainly due to the fact that I had never considered the possibility of his dying before me. That he was younger than I was, a good deal younger too, was all that ever occurred to me – as if fate paid any regard to seniority! So let us bear it constantly in mind that those we are fond of are just as liable to death as we are ourselves. What I should have said before was, 'My friend Serenus is younger than I am, but what difference does that make? He should die later than me, but it is quite possible he will die before me.' It was just because I did not do so that fortune caught me unprepared with that sudden blow. Now I bear it in mind not only that all things are liable to death but that that liability is governed by no set rules. Whatever can happen at any time can happen today. Let us reflect then, my dearest Lucilius, that we ourselves shall not be long in reaching the place we mourn his having reached. Perhaps, too, if only there is truth in the story told by sages and some welcoming abode awaits us, he whom we suppose to be dead and gone has merely been sent on ahead.

I SHARED yesterday with a bout of illness. It claimed the morning but it let me have the afternoon. So I started off by doing some reading to see what energy I had. Then, as it proved up to this, I ventured to make further demands on it – or perhaps I should say concessions to it – and did some writing. I was at this with more than my customary concentration, too, what with the difficulty of the subject and my refusal to give in, until some friends of mine put a stop to it, applying force to restrain me as if I were an invalid who was recklessly overdoing things. The pen gave place to talk, which included the following matter of dispute that I shall now state to you. We have appointed you as arbitrator – and you have more of a case on your hands than you think, for the contest is a three-cornered one.

Our Stoic philosophers, as you know, maintain that there are two elements in the universe from which all things are derived, namely cause and matter. Matter lies inert and inactive, a substance with unlimited potential, but destined to remain idle if no one sets it in motion; and it is cause (this meaning the same as reason) which turns matter to whatever end it wishes and fashions it into a variety of different products. There must, then, be something out of which things come into being and something else by means of which things come into being; the first is matter and the second is cause. Now all art is an imitation of nature. So apply what I was saying about the universe to man's handiwork. Take a statue: it had the matter to be worked on by the sculptor and it had the sculptor to give configuration to the matter – bronze, in other words, in the case of the statue, being the matter and the craftsman the cause. It is the same with all things: they consist of something which comes into being and something else which brings them into being.

Stoics believe that there is only one cause – that which brings things into being. Aristotle thinks that the term 'cause' can be used in three different ways. 'The first cause,' he says, 'is matter – without it nothing can be brought into existence. The second is the craftsman, and the third is form, which is impressed on every single piece of work as on a statue.' This last is what Aristotle calls the *idos*. 'And,' he says, 'there is a fourth as well, the purpose of the whole work.' Let me explain what this means. The 'first cause' of the statue is the bronze, as it would never have been made unless there had been something out of which it could be cast or moulded. The 'second cause' is the sculptor, as the bronze could not have been shaped into the state in which it is without those skilled hands having come to it. The 'third cause' is the form, as our statue could not have been called 'The Man with the Spear' or 'The Boy tying up his Hair'* had this not been the guise impressed on it. The 'fourth cause' is the end in view in its making, for had this not existed the statue would never have been made at all. What is this end? It is what attracted the sculptor, what his goal was in creating it: it may have been money, if when he worked it he was going to sell it, or fame, if the aim of his endeavours was to win a name, or religion, if it was a work for presentation to a temple. This too, then, is a cause of the statue's coming into being – unless you take the view that things in the absence of which the statue would never have been created should not be included among the causes of the particular creation.

To these four causes Plato adds a fifth in the model – what he himself calls the *idea* – this being what the sculptor had constantly before his eyes as he executed the intended work.

* Well-known works of Polycletus, the great fifth century Greek sculptor. Copies of both statues have survived.

It does not matter whether he has his model without, one to which he can direct his eyes, or within, conceived and set up by the artist inside his own head. God has within himself models like this of everything in the universe, his mind embracing the designs and calculations for his projects; he is full of these images which Plato calls *ideas*, eternal, immutable, ever dynamic. So though human beings may perish, humanity in itself – the pattern on which every human being is moulded – lasts on, and while human beings go through much and pass away itself remains quite unaffected. As Plato has it, then, there are five causes: the material, the agent, the form, the model and the end; and finally we get the result of all these. In the case of the statue, to use the example we began with, the material is the bronze, the agent is the sculptor, the form is the guise it is given, the model is what the sculptor making it copies, the end is what the maker has in view, and the final result is the statue itself. The universe as well, according to Plato, has all these elements. The maker is God; matter is the material; the form is the general character and lay-out of the universe as we see it; the model naturally enough is the pattern which God adopted for the creation of this stupendous work in all its beauty; the end is what God had in view when he created it, and that – in case you are asking what is the end God has in view – is goodness. That at any rate is what Plato says: 'What was the cause of God's creating the universe? He is good, and whoever is good can never be grudging with anything good; so he made it as good a world as it was in his power to make it.'

Now it is for you as judge to pronounce your verdict and declare whose statement in your opinion seems to be – not the truest (for that here is as far out of our reach as Truth herself) – but most like the truth.

This assortment of causes which Aristotle and Plato have collected together embraces either too much or too little. For if they take the view that everything in the absence of which a thing cannot be brought into being is a cause of its creation, they have failed to name enough. They should be including time in their list of causes – nothing can come into being without time. They should be including place – a thing will certainly not come into being if there is nowhere for this to happen. They should be including motion – without this nothing either comes into existence or goes out of existence; without motion there is no such thing as art and no such thing as change. What we are looking for at the moment is a primary and general cause. And this must be something elementary, since matter too is elementary. If we ask what cause is, surely the answer is creative reason, that is to say God. All those things which you have listed are not an array of individual causes, but dependent on a single one, the cause that actually creates. You may say form is a cause, but form is something which the artist imposes on his work – a part of the cause, yes, but not a cause. The model, too, is an indispensable instrument of the cause, but not a cause. To the sculptor his model is as indispensable as his chisel or his file: his art can get nowhere without them, but this does not make them parts or causes of the art. 'The end the artist has in view,' our friend says, 'the thing which induces him to set about a work of creation, is a cause.' Even if we grant that it is, it is only an accessory cause, not the effective cause. Accessory causes are infinite in number; what we are after is the general cause. In any event that assertion on the part of Plato and Aristotle that the universe in its entirety, the whole, completed work of creation, is a cause is not in keeping with their usual acuteness as thinkers. There is a very great difference between a creation and its cause.

Now you must either pronounce your verdict or – the easier course in matters of this nature – declare your inability to arrive at one and order a rehearing. 'What pleasure,' you may say, 'do you get out of frittering time away discussing those questions? It's not as if you could say they rid you of any emotion or drive out any desire.' Well, in raising and arguing these less deserving topics my own attitude is that they serve to calm the spirit, and that whilst I examine myself first, certainly, I examine the universe around me afterwards. I am not even wasting time, as you suppose, at the moment. For those questions, provided they are not subjected to a mincing or dissection with the useless kind of oversubtlety we have just seen as the result, all elevate and lighten the spirit, the soul which yearns to win free of the heavy load it is saddled with here and return to the world where it once belonged. For to it this body of ours is a burden and a torment. And harassed by the body's overwhelming weight, the soul is in captivity unless philosophy comes to its rescue, bidding it breathe more freely in the contemplation of nature, releasing it from earthly into heavenly surroundings. This to the soul means freedom, the ability to wander far and free; it steals away for a while from the prison in which it is confined and has its strength renewed in the world above. When craftsmen engaged on some intricate piece of work which imposes a tiring strain on the eyes have to work by an inadequate and undependable light, they go out into the open air and treat their eyes to the free sunshine in some open space or other dedicated to public recreation. In the same way the soul, shut away in this dim and dismal dwelling, as often as it can makes for the open and finds its relaxation in contemplating the natural universe. The wise man and devotee of philosophy is needless to say inseparable from his body, and yet he is detached from it so far as the best part of his personality is concerned, directing his thoughts towards things far above. He looks on this present life of his, much like the man who has signed on as a soldier, as the term he has to serve out. And he is so made that he neither loves life nor hates it.

He endures the lot of mortality even though he knows there is a finer one in store for him.

Are you telling me not to investigate the natural world? Are you trying to bar me from the whole of it and restrict me to a part of it? Am I not to inquire how everything in the universe began, who gave things form, who separated them out when they were all plunged together in a single great conglomeration of inert matter? Am I not to inquire into the identity of the artist who created that universe? Or the process by which this huge mass became subject to law and order? Or the nature of the one who collected the things that were scattered apart, sorted apart the things that were commingled, and when all things lay in formless chaos allotted them their individual shapes? Or the source of the light (is it fire or is it something brighter?) that is shed on us in such abundance? Am I supposed not to inquire into this sort of thing? Am I not to know where I am descended from, whether I am to see this world only once or be born into it again time after time, what my destination is to be after my stay here, what abode will await my soul on its release from the terms of its serfdom on earth? Are you forbidding me to associate with heaven, in other words ordering me to go through life with my eyes bent on the ground? I am too great, was born to too great a destiny to be my body's slave. So far as I am concerned that body is nothing more or less than a fetter on my freedom. I place it squarely in the path of fortune, letting her expend her onslaught on it, not allowing any blow to get through it to my actual self. For that body is all that is vulnerable about me: within this dwelling so liable to injury there lives a spirit that is free. Never shall that flesh compel me to feel fear, never shall it drive me to any pretence unworthy of a good man; never shall I tell a lie out of consideration for this petty body. I shall dissolve our partnership when this seems the proper course, and even now while we are bound one to the other the partnership will not be on equal terms: the soul will assume undivided authority. Refusal to be influenced by one's body assures one's freedom.

And to this freedom (to get back to the subject) even the kind of inquiries we were talking about just now have a considerable contribution to make. We know that everything in the universe is composed of matter and of God. God, encompassed within them, controls them all, they following his leadership and guidance. Greater power and greater value reside in that which creates (in this case God) than in the matter on which God works. Well, the place which in this universe is occupied by God is in man the place of the spirit. What matter is in the universe the body is in us. Let the worse, then, serve the better. Let us meet with bravery whatever may befall us. Let us never feel a shudder at the thought of being wounded or of being made a prisoner, or of poverty or persecution. What is death? Either a transition or an end. I am not afraid of coming to an end, this being the same as never having begun, nor of transition, for I shall never be in confinement quite so cramped anywhere else as I am here.

LETTER LXXVII

TODAY we saw some boats from Alexandria – the ones they call 'the mail packets' – come into view all of a sudden. They were the ones which are normally sent ahead to announce the coming of the fleet that will arrive behind them. The sight of them is always a welcome one to the Campanians. The whole of Puteoli crowded onto the wharves, all picking out the Alexandrian vessels from an immense crowd of other shipping by the actual trim of their sails, these boats being the only vessels allowed to keep their topsails spread. Out at sea all ships carry these sails, for nothing makes quite the same contribution to speed as the upper canvas, the area from which a boat derives the greatest part of its propulsion. That is why whenever the wind stiffens and becomes unduly strong sail is shortened, the wind having less force lower down. On entering the channel between Capri and the headland from which

> Upon the storm-swept summit Pallas keeps
> Her high lookout,*

regulations require all other vessels to confine themselves to carrying a mainsail, and the topsail is accordingly conspicuous on the Alexandrian boats.

While everyone around me was hurrying thus from all directions to the waterfront, I found a great deal of pleasure in refusing to bestir myself. Although there would be letters for me from my people over there I was in no hurry to know what reports they might be carrying or what might be the state of my financial interests there. For a long time now I have not been concerned about any profit or loss. This particular pleasure was one that I ought to have been experiencing even if I were not an old man; but being old in fact made it all the greater, for it meant that however little money I might have I should still have more left to cover the journey than distance left to be covered – especially as the journey on which we have all set out is one which does not have to be travelled to the very end. An ordinary journey will be incomplete if you come to a stop in the middle of it, or anywhere short of your destination, but life is never incomplete if it is an honourable one. At whatever point you leave life, if you leave it in the right way, it is a whole. And there are many occasions on which a man should leave life not only bravely but for reasons which are not as pressing as they might be – the reasons which restrain us being not so pressing either.

* The source of this quotation is not known.

Tullius Marcellinus, whom you knew very well, a man, old before his years, who found tranquillity early in life, began to meditate suicide after he had gone down with a disease which was not an incurable one but at the same time was a protracted, troublesome one, importunate in its demands. He called together a large number of his friends, and each one offered him advice. This consisted either of urgings (from the timid among them) that he should just take whichever course he himself felt urged to take, or of whatever counsel flattering admirers thought would be most likely to gratify someone meditating suicide, until a Stoic friend of mine, an outstanding personality for whom I can find no more fitting compliment than that of calling him a man of fighting courage, gave what I thought was the most inspiring advice. This was how he began: 'My dear Marcellinus,' he said, 'you mustn't let this worry you as if you were having to make a great decision. There's nothing so very great about living – all your slaves and all the animals do it. What is, however, a great thing is to die in a manner which is honourable, enlightened and courageous. Think how long now you've been doing the same as them – food, sleep, sex, the never-ending cycle. The desire for death can be experienced not merely by the enlightened or the brave or the unhappy, but even by the squeamish.' Well, Marcellinus wanted no urging, only a helper. His slaves refused to obey him in this, whereupon our Stoic talked away their fears, letting them know that the household staff could only be in danger if there had been any room for doubt as to whether their master's death had been a voluntary one; besides, he told them, it was just as bad to let other people see you ordering your master not to kill himself as actually to kill him. He then suggested to Marcellinus himself that it would not be an unkind gesture if, in the same way as at the end of a dinner the leftovers are divided among the attendants, something were offered at the end of his life to those who had served throughout it. Marcellinus had a generous and good-natured disposition which was no less evident where it meant personal expense, and he distributed accordingly little sums of money among his slaves, who were now in tears, and went out of his way to comfort them all. He did not need to resort to a weapon or to shedding blood. After going without food for three days he had a steam tent put up, in his own bedroom; a bath was brought in, in which he lay for a long time, and as fresh supplies of hot water were continually poured in he passed almost imperceptibly away, not without, as he commented more than once, a kind of pleasurable sensation, one that is apt to be produced by the gentle fading out of which those of us who have ever fainted will have some experience.

I have digressed, but you will not have minded hearing this story, since you will gather from it that your friend's departure was not a difficult or unhappy one. Although his death was self-inflicted, the manner of his passing was supremely relaxed, a mere gliding out of life. Yet the story is not without its practical value for the future. For frequently enough necessity demands just such examples. The times are frequent enough when we cannot reconcile ourselves to dying, or to knowing that we ought to die.

No one is so ignorant as not to know that some day he must die. Nevertheless when death draws near he turns, wailing and trembling, looking for a way out. Wouldn't you think a man an utter fool if he burst into tears because he didn't live a thousand years ago? A man is as much a fool for shedding tears because he isn't going to be alive a thousand years from now. There's no difference between the one and the other – you didn't exist and you won't exist – you've no concern with either period. This is the moment you've been pitched into – supposing you were to make it longer how

long would you make it? What's the point of tears? What's
the point of prayers? You're only wasting your breath.

> So give up hoping that your prayers can bring
> Some change in the decisions of the gods.*

Those decisions are fixed and permanent, part of the mighty
and eternal train of destiny. You will go the way that all
things go. What is strange about that? This is the law to
which you were born; it was the lot of your father, your
mother, your ancestors and of all who came before you as it
will be of all who come after you. There is no means of altering the irresistible succession of events which carries all
things along in its binding grip. Think of the multitudes of
people doomed to die that will be following you, that will be
keeping you company! I imagine you'd be braver about it if
thousands upon thousands were dying with you: the fact is
that men as well as other creatures are breathing their last in
one way or another in just such numbers at the very instant
when you're unable to make your mind up about death. You
weren't thinking, surely, that you wouldn't yourself one day
arrive at the destination towards which you've been heading
from the beginning? Every journey has its end.

Here I imagine you'll be expecting me to tell you the
stories of examples set by heroic men? Well, I'll tell you about
ones which children have set. History relates the story of the
famous Spartan, a mere boy who, when he was taken prisoner,
kept shouting in his native Doric, 'I shall not be a slave!' He
was as good as his word. The first time he was ordered to
perform a slave's task, some humiliating household job (his
actual orders were to fetch a disgusting chamber pot), he
dashed his head against a wall and cracked his skull open.
Freedom is as near as that – is anyone really still a slave?[54]
Would you not rather your own son died like that than lived

* Virgil, *Aeneid*, VI: 376.

by reason of spinelessness to an advanced age? Why be perturbed, then, about death when even a child can meet it bravely? Suppose you refuse to follow him: you will just be dragged after him. Assume the authority which at present lies with others. Surely you can adopt the spirited attitude of that boy and say, 'No slave am I!' At present, you unhappy creature, slave you are, slave to your fellow-men, slave to circumstance and slave to life (for life itself is slavery if the courage to die be absent).

Have you anything that might induce you to wait? You have exhausted the very pleasures that make you hesitate and hold you back; not one of them has any novelty for you, not one of them now fails to bore you out of sheer excess. You know what wine or honey-wine tastes like: it makes no difference whether a hundred or a thousand flagons go through your bladder – all you are is a strainer. You are perfectly familiar with the taste of oysters or mullet. Your luxurious way of life has kept back not a single fresh experience for you to try in coming years. And yet these are the things from which you are reluctant to be torn away. What else is there which you would be sorry to be deprived of? Friends? Do you know how to be a friend? Your country? Do you really value her so highly that you would put off your dinner for her? The sunlight? If you could you would put out that light – for what have you ever done that deserved a place in it? Confess it – it is no attachment to the world of politics or business, or even the world of nature, that makes you put off dying – the delicatessens, in which there is nothing you have left untried, are what you are reluctant to leave. You are scared of death – but how magnificently heedless of it you are while you are dealing with a dish of choice mushrooms! You want to live – but do you know how to live? You are scared of dying – and, tell me, is the kind of life you lead really any different from being dead? Caligula was once passing a column of captives on the Latin Road when one of them, with a hoary old beard reaching down his breast, begged to be put to death. 'So,' replied Caligula, 'you are alive, then, as you are?' That is the answer to give to people to whom death would actually come as a release. 'You are scared of dying? So you are alive, then, as you are?'

Someone, though, will say, 'But I want to live because of all the worthy activities I'm engaged in. I'm performing life's duties conscientiously and energetically and I'm reluctant to leave them undone.' Come now, surely you know that dying is also one of life's duties? You're leaving no duty undone, for there's no fixed number of duties laid down which you're supposed to complete. Every life without exception is a short one. Looked at in relation to the universe even the lives of Nestor and Sattia were short. In Sattia, who ordered that her epitaph should record that she had lived to the age of ninety-nine, you have an example of someone actually boasting of a prolonged old age – had it so happened that she had lasted out the hundredth year everybody, surely, would have found her quite insufferable! As it is with a play, so it is with life – what matters is not how long the acting lasts, but how good it is. It is not important at what point you stop. Stop wherever you will – only make sure that you round it off with a good ending.

LETTER LXXVIII

I AM all the more sorry to hear of the trouble you are having with constant catarrh, and the spells of feverishness which go with it when it becomes protracted to the point of being chronic, because this kind of ill health is something I have experienced myself. In its early stages I refused to let it bother me, being still young enough then to adopt a defiant attitude to sickness and put up with hardships, but eventually I succumbed to it altogether. Reduced to a state of complete emaciation, I had arrived at a point where the catarrhal discharges were virtually carrying me away with them altogether. On many an occasion I felt an urge to cut my life short there and then, and was only held back by the thought of my father, who had been the kindest of fathers to me and was then in his old age. Having in mind not how bravely I was capable of dying but how far from bravely he was capable of bearing the loss, I commanded myself to live. There are times when even to live is an act of bravery.

Let me tell you the things that provided me with consolation in those days, telling you to begin with that the thoughts which brought me this peace of mind had all the effect of medical treatment. Comforting thoughts (provided they are not of a discreditable kind) contribute to a person's cure; anything which raises his spirits benefits him physically as well. It was my Stoic studies that really saved me. For the fact that I was able to leave my bed and was restored to health I give the credit to philosophy. I owe her – and it is the least of my obligations to her – my life. But my friends also made a considerable contribution to my return to health. I found a great deal of relief in their cheering remarks, in the hours they spent at my bedside and in their conversations with me. There is nothing, my good Lucilius, quite like the devotion of one's friends for supporting one in illness and restoring one to health, or for dispelling one's anticipation and dread of death. I even came to feel that I could not really die when these were the people I would leave surviving me, or perhaps I should say I came to think I would continue to live because of them, if not among them; for it seemed to me that in death I would not be passing away but passing on my spirit to them. These things gave me the willingness to help my own recovery and to endure all the pain. It is quite pathetic, after all, if one has put the will to die behind one, to be without the will to live.

There, then, are your remedies. The doctor will be telling you how much walking you should do, how much exercise you should take; he will be telling you not to overdo the inactivity – as is the tendency with invalids – and recommending reading aloud to exercise the breathing (its passages and reservoir being the areas affected); he will recommend that you take a trip by sea and derive some stimulation for the internal organs from the gentle motion of the boat; he will prescribe a diet for you, and tell you when to make use of wine as a restorative and when to give it up in case it starts you coughing or aggravates your cough. My own advice to you – and not only in the present illness but in your whole life as well – is this: refuse to let the thought of death bother you: nothing is grim when we have escaped that fear. There are three upsetting things about any illness: the fear of dying, the physical suffering and the interruption of our pleasures. I have said enough about the first, but will just say this, that the fear is due to the facts of nature, not of illness. Illness has actually given many people a new lease of life; the experience of being near to death has been their preservation. You will die not because you are sick but because you are alive. That end still awaits you when you have been cured. In getting well again you may be escaping some ill health but not death. Now let us go back and deal with the disadvantage which really does belong to illness, the fact that it involves considerable physical torments. These are made bearable by their inter-mittency. For when pain is at its most severe the very intensity finds means of ending it. Nobody can be in acute pain and feel it for long. Nature in her unlimited kindness to us has so arranged things as to make pain either bearable or brief. The severest pains have their seat in the most attenuated parts of the body; any area of slight dimensions like a tendon or a joint causes excruciating agony when trouble arises within its small confines. But these parts of our anatomy go numb very quickly, the pain itself giving rise to a loss of all sensation of pain (either because the life force is impaired by being held up in its natural circulation and so loses its active power, the power which enables it to give us warning of pain, or because the diseased secretions, no longer able to drain away, become self-obliterated and deprive the areas they have congested of sensation). Thus gout in the feet or the hands or any pain in the vertebrae or tendons has intermittent lulls when it has dulled the area it is torturing; these are all cases in which the distress is caused by the initial twinges and the violence of the pain disappears as time goes on, the suffering ending in a state of insensibility. The reason why pain in an eye, an ear or a tooth is exceptionally severe is the fact that it develops in a limited area, and indeed this applies just as much to pains in the head; nevertheless if its intensity goes beyond a certain point it is turned into a state of dazed stupefaction. So there is the comforting thing about extremities of pain: if you feel it too much you are bound to stop feeling it.

What in fact makes people who are morally unenlightened upset by the experience of physical distress is their failure to acquire the habit of contentment with the spirit. They have instead been preoccupied by the body. That is why a man of noble and enlightened character separates body from spirit and has just as much to do with the former, the frail and complaining part of our nature, as is necessary and no more, and a lot to do with the better, the divine element. 'But it's hard having to do without pleasures we're used to, having to give up food and go thirsty as well as hungry.' Tiresome it is in the first stages of abstinence. Later, as the organs of appetite decline in strength with exhaustion, the cravings die down;

·thereafter the stomach becomes fussy, unable to stand things it could never have enough of before. The desires themselves die away. And there is nothing harsh about having to do without things for which you have ceased to have any craving.

Another point is that every pain leaves off altogether, or at least falls off in intensity, from time to time. Moreover one can guard against its arrival and employ drugs to forestall it just as it is coming on; for every pain (or at least every pain with a habit of regular recurrence) gives one advance warning of its coming. In illness the suffering is always bearable so long as you refuse to be affected by the ultimate threat.

So do not go out of your way to make your troubles any more tiresome than they are and burden yourself with fretting. Provided that one's thinking has not been adding anything to it, pain is a trivial sort of thing. If by contrast you start giving yourself encouragement, saying to yourself, 'It's nothing – or nothing much, anyway – let's stick it out, it'll be over presently', then in thinking it a trivial matter you will be ensuring that it actually is. Everything hangs on one's thinking. The love of power or money or luxurious living are not the only things which are guided by popular thinking. We take our cue from people's thinking even in the way we feel pain.

A man is as unhappy as he has convinced himself he is. And complaining away about one's sufferings after they are over (you know the kind of language: 'No one had ever been in such a bad state. The torments and hardships I endured! No one thought I would recover. The number of times I was given up for lost by the family! The number of times I was despaired of by the doctors! A man on the rack isn't torn with pain the way I was') is something I think should be banned. Even if all this is true, it is past history. What's the good of dragging up sufferings which are over, of being unhappy now

just because you were then? What is more, doesn't everyone
add a good deal to his tale of hardships and deceive himself as
well in the matter? Besides, there is a pleasure in having succeeded in enduring something the actual enduring of which
was very far from pleasant; when some trouble or other
comes to an end the natural thing is to be glad. There are
two things, then, the recollecting of trouble in the past as
well as the fear of troubles to come, that I have to root out:
the first is no longer of any concern to me and the second has
yet to be so. And when a man is in the grip of difficulties he
should say

> There may be pleasure in the memory
> Of even these events one day.*

He should put his whole heart into the fight against them. If
he gives way before them he will lose the battle; if he exerts
himself against them he will win. What in fact most people do
is pull down on their own heads what they should be holding
up against; when something is in imminent danger of falling
on you, the pressure of it bearing heavily on you, it will only
move after you and become an even greater weight to support if you back away from it; if instead you stand your
ground, willing yourself to resist, it will be forced back.
Look at the amount of punishment that boxers and wrestlers
take to the face and the body generally! They will put up
none the less with any suffering in their desire for fame, and
will undergo it all not merely in the course of fighting but
in preparing for their fights as well: their training in itself
constitutes suffering. Let us too overcome all things, with
our reward consisting not in any wreath or garland, not in
trumpet-calls for silence for the ceremonial proclamation of
our name, but in moral worth, in strength of spirit, in a

* Virgil, *Aeneid*, I:203.

peace that is won for ever once in any contest fortune has been utterly defeated.

'I'm suffering severe pain,' you may say. Well does it stop you suffering it if you endure it in a womanish fashion? In the same way as the enemy can do far more damage to your army if it is in full retreat, every trouble that may come our way presses harder on the one who has turned tail and is giving ground. 'But it's really severe.' Well, is courage only meant to enable us to bear up under what is not severe? Would you rather have an illness that's long drawn out or one that's short and quick? If it's a long one it will have the odd interval, giving one opportunity for rallying, granting one a good deal of time free of it, having of necessity to pause in order to build up again. An illness that's swift and short will have one of two results: either oneself or it will be snuffed out. And what difference does it make whether I or it disappears? Either way there's an end to the pain.

Another thing which will help is to turn your mind to other thoughts and that way get away from your suffering. Call to mind things which you have done that have been upright or courageous; run over in your mind the finest parts that you have played. And cast your memory over the things you have most admired; this is a time for recollecting all those individuals of exceptional courage who have triumphed over pain: the man who steadily went on reading a book while he was having varicose veins cut out: the man who never stopped smiling under torture albeit that this angered his tormentors into trying on him every instrument of cruelty they had. If pain has been conquered by a smile will it not be conquered by reason? And here you may mention anything you care to name, catarrh, a fit of uninterrupted*coughing so violent that it brings up parts of the internal organs, having one's very entrails seared by a fever, thirst, having limbs wrenched in different directions with dislocation of the joints, or – worse than these – being stretched on the rack or burnt alive, or subjected to the red-hot plates and instruments designed to re-open and deepen swelling wounds. There have been men who have undergone these experiences and never uttered a groan. 'He needs more, he hasn't asked for mercy . . . he needs more, he still hasn't answered . . . he needs more, he has actually smiled, and not a forced smile either.' Surely pain is something you will want to smile at after this.

'But my illness has taken me away from my duties and won't allow me to achieve anything.' It is your body, not your mind as well, that is in the grip of ill health. Hence it may slow the feet of a runner and make the hands of a smith or cobbler less efficient, but if your mind is by habit of an active turn you may still give instruction and advice, listen and learn, inquire and remember. Besides, if you meet sickness in a sensible manner, do you really think you are achieving nothing? You will be demonstrating that even if one cannot always beat it one can always bear an illness. There is room for heroism, I assure you, in bed as anywhere else. War and the battle-front are not the only spheres in which proof is to be had of a spirited and fearless character: a person's bravery is no less evident under the bed-clothes. There is something it lies open to you to achieve, and that is making the fight with illness a good one. If its threats or importunities leave you quite unmoved, you are setting others a signal example. How much scope there would be for re-nown if whenever we were sick we had an audience of specta-tors! Be your own spectator anyway, your own applauding audience.

Pleasures, moreover, are of two kinds. The physical pleas-ures are the ones which illness interferes with, though it does not do away with them altogether – indeed, if you take a true view of the matter, they are actually sharpened by illness, a man deriving greater pleasure from drinking something when he is thirsty and finding food all the more welcome through being hungry, anything set before one after one has had to fast being greeted with a heightened appetite. But no doctor can refuse his patient those other, greater and surer pleasures, the pleasures of the mind and spirit. Anyone who follows these and genuinely knows them pays no attention whatever to all the enticements of the senses. 'How very unfortunate he is,' people say, 'to be sick like that!' Why? Because he isn't melting snow in his wine? Because he isn't breaking ice into a bumper goblet to keep the drink he has mixed in it chilled? Because Lucrine oysters aren't being opened before him at his table? Because there isn't any bust-ling of cooks about the dining-room, bringing in not just the viands themselves but the actual cooking apparatus along with them? For this is the latest innovation in luxurious living, having the kitchen accompany the dinner in to the table so as to prevent any of the food losing its heat and avoid anything being at a temperature insufficiently scalding for palates which are nowadays like leather. 'How very unfortunate he is to be sick,' they say. In fact he'll be eating just as much as he'll digest. There won't be a whole boar lying somewhere where people can see it, conveying the impression that it has been banished from the table as being too cheap and ordinary a piece of meat to be on it, nor will he have his trolley piled high with – now that people think it not quite nice to see the whole bird – carved breast of fowl. And what's so bad about your being deprived of that? You may be eating like a sick man, but you'll at last be eating in the way a healthy man should.

But given one thing we shall find it easy to put up with the potions and warm drinks and all the rest of it – all the things that seem unbearable to people who have become spoilt, who have become soft through a life of luxury, ailing more in the mind than they ever are in the body; the one requirement is that we cease to dread death. And so we shall as soon as we have learnt to distinguish the good things and the bad things in this world. Then and then only shall we stop being weary of living as well as scared of dying. For a life spent viewing all the variety, the majesty, the sublimity in things around us can never succumb to *ennui*: the feeling that one is tired of being, of existing, is usually the result of an idle and inactive leisure. Truth will never pall on someone who explores the world of nature, wearied as a person will be by the spurious things. Moreover, even if death is on the way with a summons for him, though it come all too early, though it cut him off in the prime of life, he has experienced every reward that the very longest life can offer, having gained extensive knowledge of the world we live in, having learnt that time adds nothing to the finer things in life. Whereas any life must needs seem short to people who measure it in terms of pleasures which through their empty nature are incapable of completeness.

Let these reflections promote your recovery, and meanwhile do find time for our correspondence. Time will bring us together again one of these days; and when, as it will, the reunion comes, however short it may last, knowing how to make the most of it will turn it into a long one. As Posidonius said, 'In a single day there lies open to men of learning more than there ever does to the unenlightened in the longest of lifetimes.' In the meantime cling tooth and nail to the following rule: not to give in to adversity, never to trust prosperity, and always take full note of fortune's habit of behaving just as she pleases, treating her as if she were actually going to do everything it is in her power to do. Whatever you have been expecting for some time comes as less of a shock.

LETTER LXXXIII

YOU demand an account of my days – generally as well as individually. You think well of me if you suppose that there is nothing in them for me to hide. And we should, indeed, live as if we were in public view, and think, too, as if someone could peer into the inmost recesses of our hearts – which someone can! For what is to be gained if something is concealed from man when nothing is barred from God? He is present in our minds, in attendance in the midst of our thoughts – although by 'attendance' I do not mean to suggest that he is not at times absent from our thoughts. I shall do as you say, then, and gladly give you a record of what I do and in what order. I shall put myself under observation straight away and undertake a review of my day – a course which is of the utmost benefit. What really ruins our characters is the fact that none of us looks back over his life. We think about what we are going to do, and only rarely of that, and fail to think about what we have done, yet any plans for the future are dependent on the past.

Today has been unbroken. No one has robbed me of any part of it. It has been wholly divided between my bed and my reading. A very small part of it has been given over to physical exercise – and on this account I'm grateful for old age, for the exercise costs me little trouble. I only have to stir and I'm weary, and that after all is the end of exercise even for the strongest. Interested in having my trainers? One's enough for me – Pharius, a likeable young fellow, as you know, but he's due for a change. I'm looking now for someone rather more youthful. He in fact declares that we're both at the same climacteric since we're both losing our teeth. But I've reached the stage where I can only keep up with him with difficulty when we're out for a run, and before many days are out I won't be able to keep up with him at all. See what daily exercise does for one. When two people are going in opposite directions there's soon a big distance between them: he's coming up at the same time as I'm going downwards, and you know how much quicker travel is in the second of these directions. But I'm wrong: the age I'm at isn't one that is 'going downwards' – it's one that's in headlong descent.

However, you'd like to hear how today's race ended? Well, we made it a tie, something that doesn't often happen with runners. After this, more a spell of exhaustion than of exercise, I had a cold plunge – cold, with me, meaning just short of warm! Here I am, once celebrated as a devotee of cold baths, regularly paying my respects to the Canal on the first of January and jumping into the Maiden Pool in just the same way as I read, wrote and spoke some sentence or other every New Year in order to ensure good luck in the coming year; and now I've shifted my scene of operations, first to the Tiber, then to my own pool here, which, even when I'm feeling my heartiest and don't cheat, has had the chill taken off it by the sun; it's a short step to a hot bath! The next thing is breakfast, which consists of some dry bread; no table laid, and no need to wash the hands after such a meal. I then have the briefest of naps. You know this habit of mine, of dropping off for a moment or two, just slipping off the harness, as you might say. I find it enough to have simply stopped being awake. Sometimes I know I've been asleep, sometimes merely guess I have been. . . .*

Zeno was a very great man as well as the founder of our Stoic school, a school with an unequalled record for courageous and saintly living; well, listen to the way in which,

* A total of about 85 lines of this letter have been omitted as not of interest or repeating thoughts expressed elsewhere.

desiring to deter us from drunkenness, he deduces the principle that the good man won't get drunk. 'No person who is drunk,' he says, 'is entrusted with a secret: the good man is entrusted with a secret: therefore, the good man will not get drunk.' Watch how ridiculous he's made to look when we counter with a single syllogism on the same pattern (of the many we could advance it's sufficient to instance one). 'No person who is asleep is entrusted with a secret: the good man is entrusted with a secret: therefore, the good man does not go to sleep. . . .'

Now just let each of us name for himself the people he knows can be trusted with a secret though they can't be trusted with a bottle. I'll give, all the same, one solitary example myself, just to prevent its being lost to human memory! Life needs a stock of noteworthy examples; nor need we always go running to antiquity for them. Lucius Piso was drunk from the very moment of his appointment as Warden of the City of Rome. He regularly spent most of the night wining and dining in company, and slept from then until around midday, noon to him being early morning; he nevertheless discharged his duties, which embraced the general welfare of the whole city, with the utmost efficiency. The late emperor Augustus as well as Tiberius entrusted him with secret orders, the former on appointing him governor of Thrace (the conquest of which he completed), the latter when he left Rome for Campania, leaving behind him in the capital many objects of distrust and hostility. I imagine it was because Piso's drunken habits had been such a success so far as he was concerned that Tiberius later appointed Cossus to be Prefect of the City. This man, otherwise dignified and self-controlled, steeped himself in liquor, soaking it up to such an extent that on one occasion in the Senate, having come there straight from a party, he succumbed to a slumber from which nothing could rouse him and had to be carried out. Yet this did not stop Tiberius writing (in his own hand) a number of letters to Cossus the contents of which he did not consider suitable for communication even to his ministers; and Cossus never let slip a single secret, whether private or official. . . .

If you want to arrive at the conclusion that the good man ought not to get drunk, why set about it with syllogisms? Tell people how disgusting it is for a man to pump more into himself than he can hold and not to know the capacity of his own stomach. Tell them of all the things men do that they would blush at sober, and that drunkenness is nothing but a state of self-induced insanity. For imagine the drunken man's behaviour extended over several days: would you hesitate to think him out of his mind? As it is, the difference is simply one of duration, not of degree. Point to the example of Alexander of Macedon, stabbing his dearest and truest friend, Clitus, at a banquet, and wanting to die, as indeed he should have done, when he realized the enormity of what he had done. Drunkenness inflames and lays bare every vice, removing the reserve that acts as a check on impulses to wrong behaviour. For people abstain from forbidden things far more often through feelings of inhibition when it comes to doing what is wrong than through any will to good. . . . Add to this the drunkard's ignorance of his situation, his indistinct, uncertain speech, his inability to walk straight, his unsteady eye and swimming head, with his very home in a state of motion – as if the whole house had been set spinning by some cyclone – and the tortures in his stomach as the wine ferments. . . .

Where is the glory in mere capacity? When the victory rests with you, when all the company lie prostrate around you, slumbering or vomiting, declining all your calls for another toast, when you find yourself the only person at the party still on your feet, when your mighty prowess has enabled you to beat all comers and no one has proved able to match your intake, a barrel is none the less enough to beat you.

What else was it but drinking to excess, together with a passion for Cleopatra itself as potent as drink, that ruined that great and gifted man, Mark Antony, dragging him down into foreign ways of living and un-Roman vices? This it was that made him an enemy of the state; this is what made him no match for his enemies; it was this that made him cruel, having the heads of his country's leading men brought in to him at the dinner-table, identifying the hands and features of liquidated opponents in the course of banquets marked by sumptuous magnificence and regal pomp, still thirsting for blood when filled to the full with wine. ...

Explain, then, why the good man should avoid getting drunk, using facts, not words, to show its ugliness and offensiveness. Prove – and an easy task it is – that so-called pleasures, when they go beyond a certain limit, are but punishments. ...

LETTER LXXXVI

HERE I am, staying at the country house which once belonged to Scipio of Africa himself. I am writing after paying my respects to his departed spirit as well as to an altar which I rather think may be the actual tomb of that great soldier. His soul will have gone to heaven, returned in fact to the place from which it came. What convinces me of this is not the size of the armies he commanded – for Cambyses equally had such armies and Cambyses was merely a madman who turned his madness to good account – but his quite exceptional self-restraint and sense of duty. This is something in him which I find even more deserving of admiration at the time when he finally left his country than during the time when he was fighting for her. Was Scipio to stay in Rome? Or was Rome to stay a free democracy? That was then the choice. What did Scipio say? 'I have no wish,' he said, 'to have the effect of weakening in the least degree our laws or institutions. All Roman citizens must be equal before the law. I ask my country, then, to make the most of what I have done for her, but without me. If she owes it to me that she is today a free country, let me also prove that she is free. If my stature has grown too great for her best interests, then out I go.' Am I not justified in admiring that nobility of character which led him to retire, to go into voluntary exile to relieve the state of an embarrassing burden? Events had come to the point where either Scipio or democracy was going to suffer at the other's hands. Neither of these two things could justly be permitted to happen. So he gave way to her constitution and, proposing that the nation should be no less indebted to him for *his* absence from the scene than for Hannibal's, he went off into retirement at Liternum.

I have seen the house, which is built of squared stone blocks; the wall surrounding the park; and the towers built out on both sides of the house for purposes of defence; the well, concealed among the greenery and out-buildings, with sufficient water to provide for the needs of a whole army; and the tiny little bath, situated after the old-fashioned custom in an ill-lit corner, our ancestors believing that the only place where one could properly have a hot bath was in the dark. It was this which started in my mind reflections that occasioned me a good deal of enjoyment as I compared Scipio's way of life and our own. In this corner the famous Terror of Carthage, to whom Rome owes it that she has only once* in her history been captured, used to wash a body weary from work on the farm! For he kept himself fit through toil, cultivating his fields by his own labour, as was the regular

* By the Gauls in 390 B.C.

way in the old days. And this was the ceiling, dingy in the extreme, under which he stood; and this the equally undistinguished paving that carried his weight.

Who is there who could bear to have a bath in such surroundings nowadays? We think ourselves poorly off, living like paupers, if the walls are not ablaze with large and costly circular mirrors, if our Alexandrian marbles are not decorated with panels of Numidian marble, if the whole of their surface has not been given a decorative overlay of elaborate patterns having all the variety of fresco murals, unless the ceiling cannot be seen for glass, unless the pools into which we lower bodies with all the strength drained out of them by lengthy periods in the sweating room are edged with Thasian marble (which was once the rarest of sights even in a temple), unless the water pours from silver taps. And so far we have only been talking about the ordinary fellow's plumbing. What about the bath-houses of certain former slaves? Look at their arrays of statues, their assemblies of columns that do not support a thing but are put up purely for ornament, just for the sake of spending money. Look at the cascades of water splashing noisily down from one level to the next. We have actually come to such a pitch of choosiness that we object to walking on anything other than precious stones.

In this bathroom of Scipio's there are tiny chinks – you could hardly call them windows – pierced in the masonry of the wall in such a way as to let in light without in any way weakening its defensive character. Nowadays 'moth-hole' is the way some people speak of a bathroom unless it has been designed to catch the sun through enormous windows all day long, unless a person can acquire a tan at the same time as he is having a bath, unless he has views from the bath over countryside and sea.

The result is that bath-houses which drew admiring

crowds when they were first opened are actually dismissed as antiquated as soon as extravagance has hit on any novelty calculated to put its own best previous efforts in the shade. There was a time when bath-houses were few and far between, and never in the least luxuriously appointed – and why should they have been, considering that they were designed for use, not for diversion, and that admission only cost you a copper? There were no showers in those days, and the water did not come in a continuous gush as if from a hot spring. People did not think it mattered then how clear the water was in which they were going to get rid of the dirt. Heavens, what a pleasure it is to go into one of those half-lit bath-houses with their ordinary plastered ceilings, where you knew that Cato himself as aedile – or Fabius Maximus, or one of the Cornelii – regulated the warmth of your water with his own hand! For, however high their rank, it was one of the duties of the aediles to enter all such premises as were open to the public and enforce standards of cleanliness and a healthy sort of temperature, sufficient for practical purposes, not the kind of heat which has recently come into fashion, more like that of a furnace – so much so indeed that a slave convicted on a criminal charge might well be sentenced to be *bathed* alive! There doesn't seem to me to be any difference now between 'your bath's warm' and 'your bath's boiling'.

'How primitive!' Such is some people's verdict these days on Scipio because he did not have extensive areas of glass to let the daylight into the perspiring room, because it was not a habit with him to get himself cooked in strong sunlight in his own bathroom, letting time go by until he was perfectly done! 'Wretched man! He didn't know how to live! He'd take his bath in water that was never filtered and often cloudy, practically muddy in fact after any heavy rain.' Well, it did not make much difference to Scipio if this was the kind of bath he had; he went there to wash off sweat, not scent. And what do you think some people will say to this? 'Well, I don't envy Scipio; if that was the kind of bath he had all the time, it was a real exile's life that he was leading.'

Yes, and what's more, if you must know, he didn't even have a bath every day. Writers who have left us a record of life in ancient Rome tell us that it was just their arms and legs, which of course they dirtied working, that people washed every day, bathing all over only once a week on market day. 'Obviously,' someone will comment, 'there must have been times when they were positively disgusting.' And what do you think they stank of? I'll tell you – of hard soldiering, of hard work, of all that goes to make up a man. Men are dirtier creatures now than they ever were in the days before the coming of spotlessly clean bathrooms. What is it Horace says when he wants to describe a man noted and indeed notorious for the inordinate lengths to which he carried personal fastidiousness?

Bucillus stinks of scented lozenges.*

Produce Bucillus today and he might just as well 'stink like a goat'. He would be in the same position as the Gargonius with whom Horace contrasted him. For nowadays it is not even enough to use some scented ointment – it must be re-applied two or three times a day as a precaution against its evaporation on the person. I say nothing about the way people preen themselves on the perfume it carries, as if it were their own.

If all this strikes you as being excessively disapproving you must put it down to the house's atmosphere! During my stay in it I've learnt from Aegialus (who's the present owner of the estate, and gives a great deal of attention to its management) that trees can be transplanted even when quite old – a lesson that we old men need to learn when we reckon that every

* Horace, *Satires*, I:2.27 and I:4.92. Horace actually wrote Rufillus.

one of us who puts down a new olive plantation is doing so
for someone else's benefit – now that I've seen him carefully
transplanting one of a number of trees that had given fruit
unstintingly over three and even four seasons. So you too can
enjoy the shade of the tree which

> Is slow in coming up, is there to give
> Your grandsons shade in later years, long hence,*

according to our Virgil, who was not concerned with the
facts but with poetic effect, his object being the pleasure of
the reader, not the instruction of the farmer. To pick out
only one example, let me quote the following passage which
I felt compelled to find fault with today.

> In Spring's the time for sowing beans; then, too,
> The crumbling furrows, Clover, welcome you,
> And millet, too, receives her yearly care.†

I leave you to conclude from this whether the crops mentioned
are to be planted at the same time as each other, and whether
in each case they're to be sown in spring. As I write, it's
June, getting on for July now, too, and I've seen people
harvesting beans and sowing millet on the same day.

To get back to our olive plantation, I saw two different
methods of planting used here. In the first, taking sizeable
trees and lopping off the branches, cutting them back to a
foot from the stem, Aegialus transplanted them complete
with crown, pruning away the roots and leaving only the
actual base, the part to which the roots are attached. This he
placed in the hole with an application of manure, and not
only earthed it in but trod and stamped the soil down hard.
He says that nothing gives such good results as this 'packing
them down', as he calls it; what it does, of course, is to keep

* Virgil, *Georgics*, II:58.
† Virgil, *Georgics*, I:215–16.

out cold and wind; and apart from that, the tree is less liable to be shifted, thus allowing the young roots to sprout and get a grip on the soil when they are inevitably tender and torn from their precarious holds by the slightest disturbance. He also scrapes the crown of the tree before covering it up, because (he says) new roots emerge wherever the wood underneath has been laid bare. The tree, again, should not stand higher than three or four feet above the ground. This will ensure, right from the start, green growth from the bottom upwards instead of a large area of dry and withered stem of the sort one sees in old olive-groves.

The second method was as follows: taking branches of the type one normally finds on very young trees, strong but at the same time having soft bark, he planted them out in the same sort of way. These grow rather more slowly but since they spring from what is virtually a cutting, there is nothing scraggy or unsightly about them.

Another thing I've seen is the transplanting of an old vine from its supporting tree; in this case, one has to gather up with it, if possible, even the minute root-hairs, and in addition give it a more generous covering of soil so that it throws out roots from the stem as well. I have seen such plantings not only in the month of February but even at the end of March, the vines going on to embrace and take good hold of their new elm trees. Aegialus also says that all trees which are stout in the stem, if one may so term them, should have the benefit of a supply of water stored in tanks; if this is a success, we have brought the rain under our control.

But I don't propose to tell you any more, in case I turn you into a rival grower in the same way as Aegialus has turned me into a competitor of his!

LETTER LXXXVIII

You want to know my attitude towards liberal studies. Well, I have no respect for any study whatsoever if its end is the making of money. Such studies are to me unworthy ones. They involve the putting out of skills to hire, and are only of value in so far as they may develop the mind without occupying it for long. Time should be spent on them only so long as one's mental abilities are not up to dealing with higher things. They are our apprenticeship, not our real work. Why 'liberal studies' are so called is obvious: it is because they are the ones considered worthy of a free man.* But there is really only one liberal study that deserves the name – because it makes a person free – and that is the pursuit of wisdom. Its high ideals, its steadfastness and spirit make all other studies puerile and puny in comparison. Do you really think there is anything to be said for the others when you find among the people who profess to teach them quite the most reprehensible and worthless characters you could have as teachers? All right to have studied that sort of thing once, but not to be studying them now.

The question has sometimes been posed whether these liberal studies make a man a better person. But in fact they do not aspire to any knowledge of how to do this, let alone claim to do it. Literary scholarship concerns itself with research into language, or history if a rather broader field is preferred, or, extending its range to the very limit, poetry. Which of these paves the way to virtue? Attentiveness to words, analysis of syllables, accounts of myths, laying down the principles of prosody? What is there in all this that dispels fear, roots out desire or reins in passion? Or let us take a look at music, at geometry; you will not find anything in

* A *liber*.

151

them which tells us not to be afraid of this or desire that – and if anyone lacks this kind of knowledge all his other knowledge is valueless to him. The question is whether or not that sort of scholar is teaching virtue. For if he is not, he will not even be imparting it incidentally. If he is teaching it he is a philosopher. If you really want to know how far these persons are from the position of being moral teachers, observe the absence of connexion between all the things they study; if they were teaching one and the same thing a connexion would be evident. Unless perhaps they manage to persuade you that Homer was actually a philosopher – though they refute their case by means of the very passages which lead them to infer it. For at one moment they make him a Stoic, giving nothing but virtue his approval, steering clear of pleasure, not even an offer of immortality inducing him to stoop to the dishonourable; at another they make him an Epicurean, praising the way of life of a society passing its days at peace and ease, in an atmosphere of dinner-parties and music-making; at another he becomes a Peripatetic, with a three-fold classification of things good; at another an Academic, stating that nothing is certain. It is obvious that none of these philosophies is to be found in Homer for the very reason that they all are, the doctrines being mutually incompatible. Even suppose we grant these people that Homer was a philosopher, he became a wise man, surely, before he could recite any epics, so that what we should be learning are the things which made him wise. And there is no more point in my investigating which was the earlier, Homer or Hesiod, than there would be in my knowing the reason why Hecuba, though younger than Helen, carried her years so unsuccessfully. And what, I would ask this kind of scholar, do you suppose is the point of trying to establish the ages of Patroclus and Achilles? And are you more concerned to find out where Ulysses' wanderings took him than to find a way of putting an end to our own perpetual wanderings? We haven't the time to spare to hear whether it was between Italy and Sicily that he ran into a storm or somewhere outside the area of the world we know – wanderings as extensive as his could never in fact have taken place inside so limited an area – when every day we're running into our own storms, spiritual storms, and driven by vice into all the troubles that Ulysses ever knew. We're not spared those eye-distracting beauties, or attackers. We too have to contend in various places with savage monsters revelling in human blood, insidious voices that beguile our ears, shipwrecks and all manner of misfortune. What you should be teaching me is how I may attain such a love for my country, my father and my wife, and keep on course for those ideals even after shipwreck. Why go into the question whether or not Penelope completely took in her contemporaries and was far from being a model of wifely purity, any more than the question whether or not she had a feeling that the man she was looking at was Ulysses before she actually knew it? Teach me instead what purity is, how much value there is in it, whether it lies in the body or in the mind.

Turning to the musical scholar I say this. You teach me how bass and treble harmonize, or how strings producing different notes can give rise to concord. I would rather you brought about some harmony in my mind and got my thoughts into tune. You show me which are the plaintive keys. I would rather you showed me how to avoid uttering plaintive notes when things go against me in life.

The geometrician teaches me how to work out the size of my estates – rather than how to work out how much a man needs in order to have enough. He teaches me to calculate, putting my fingers into the service of avarice, instead of teaching me that there is no point whatsoever in that sort of computation and that a person is none the happier for having properties which tire accountants out, or to put it another way, how superfluous a man's possessions are when he would be a picture of misery if you forced him to start counting up single-handed how much he possessed. What use is it to me to be able to divide a piece of land into equal areas if I'm unable to divide it with a brother? What use is the ability to measure out a portion of an acre with an accuracy extending even to the bits which elude the measuring rod if I'm upset when some high-handed neighbour encroaches slightly on my property? The geometrician teaches me how I may avoid losing any fraction of my estates, but what I really want to learn is how to lose the lot and still keep smiling. 'But I'm being turned off the land my father and grandfather owned before me!' Well, so what? Who owned the land before your grandfather? Are you in a position to identify the community, let alone the individual, to whom it originally belonged? You entered on it as a tenant, not an absolute owner. Whose tenant, you may ask? Your heir's, and that only if you're lucky. The legal experts say that acquisition by prescription never applies where the property concerned is actually public property. Well, what you possess and call your own is really public property, or mankind's property for that matter. Oh, the marvels of geometry! You geometers can calculate the areas of circles, can reduce any given shape to a square, can state the distances separating stars. Nothing's outside your scope when it comes to measurement. Well, if you're such an expert, measure a man's soul; tell me how large or how small that is. You can define a straight line; what use is that to you if you've no idea what straightness means in life?

I come now to the person who prides himself on his familiarity with the heavenly bodies:

> Towards which quarter chilly Saturn draws,
> The orbits in which burning Mercury roams.*

* Virgil, *Georgics*, I:336–7. The person meant is of course the astrologer, not the astronomer.

What is to be gained from this sort of knowledge? Am I supposed to feel anxious when Saturn and Mars are in opposition or Mercury sets in the evening in full view of Saturn, instead of coming to learn that bodies like these are equally propitious wherever they are, and incapable of change in any case. They are swept on in a path from which they cannot escape, their motion governed by an uninterrupted sequence of destined events, making their reappearances in cycles that are fixed. They either actuate or signalize all that comes about in the universe. If every event is brought about by them, how is mere familiarity with a process which is unchangeable going to be of any help? If they are pointers to events, what difference does it make to be aware in advance of things you cannot escape? They are going to happen whether you know about them or not.

> If you observe the hasting sun and watch
> The stars processing through the skies, the day
> That follows will not prove you wrong; nor will
> Deceptive cloudfree nights then take you in.*

I've taken sufficient precautions, more than sufficient precautions, to ensure that I'm not taken in by deceptive phenomena. At this you'll protest: 'Can you really say "the day that follows never proves me wrong"? Surely anything that happens which one didn't know in advance was going to happen proves one wrong?' Well, I don't know what's going to happen; but I do know what's capable of happening – and none of this will give rise to any protest on my part. I'm ready for everything. If I'm let off in any way, I'm pleased. The day in question proves me wrong in a sense if it treats me leniently, but even so not really wrong, for just as I know that anything is capable of happening so also do I know that it's not bound to happen. So I look for the best and am prepared for the opposite.

* Virgil, *Georgics*, I:424–6.[55]

You'll have to bear with me if I digress here. Nothing will induce me to accept painters into the list of liberal arts, any more than sculptors, marble-masons and all the other attendants on extravagance. I must equally reject those oil and dust practitioners, the wrestlers, or else I shall have to include in the list the perfumers and cooks and all the others who place their talents at the service of our pleasures. What is there, I ask you, that's liberal about those characters who vomit up their food to empty their stomachs for more, with their bodies stuffed full and their minds all starved and inactive? Can we possibly look on this as a liberal accomplishment for the youth of Rome, whom our ancestors trained to stand up straight and throw a javelin, to toss the caber, and manage a horse, and handle weapons? They never used to teach their children anything which could be learned in a reclining posture. That kind of training, nevertheless, doesn't teach or foster moral values any more than the other. What's the use, after all, of mastering a horse and controlling him with the reins at full gallop if you're carried away yourself by totally unbridled emotions? What's the use of overcoming opponent after opponent in the wrestling or boxing rings if you can be overcome by your temper?

'So we don't,' you may ask, 'in fact gain anything from the liberal studies?' As far as character is concerned, no, but we gain a good deal from them in other directions – just as even these admittedly inferior arts which we've been talking about, the ones that are based on use of the hands, make important contributions to the amenities of life although they have nothing to do with character. Why then do we give our sons a liberal education? Not because it can make them morally good but because it prepares the mind for the acquisition of moral values. Just as that grounding in grammar, as they called it in the old days, in which boys are given their elementary schooling, does not teach them the liberal arts but prepares the ground for knowledge of them in due course, so when it comes to character the liberal arts open the way to it rather than carry the personality all the way there. . . . *

In this connexion I feel prompted to take a look at individual qualities of character. Bravery is the one which treats with contempt things ordinarily inspiring fear, despising and defying and demolishing all the things that terrify us and set chains on human freedom. Is she in any way fortified by liberal studies? Take loyalty, the most sacred quality that can be found in a human breast, never corrupted by a bribe, never driven to betray by any form of compulsion, crying: 'Beat me, burn me, put me to death, I shall not talk – the more the torture probes my secrets the deeper I'll hide them!' Can liberal studies create that kind of spirit? Take self-control, the quality which takes command of the pleasures; some she dismisses out of hand, unable to tolerate them; others she merely regulates, ensuring that they are brought within healthy limits; never approaching pleasures for their own sake, she realizes that the ideal limit with things you desire is not the amount you would like to but the amount you ought to take. Humanity is the quality which stops one being arrogant towards one's fellows, or being acrimonious. In words, in actions, in emotions she reveals herself as kind and good-natured towards all. To her the troubles of anyone else are her own, and anything that benefits herself she welcomes primarily because it will be of benefit to someone else. Do the liberal studies inculcate these attitudes? No, no more than they do simplicity, or modesty and restraint, or frugality and thrift, or mercy, the mercy that is as sparing with another's blood as though it were its own, knowing that it is not for man to make wasteful use of man.

Someone will ask me how I can say that liberal studies

* Some 45 lines of the Latin are omitted for their relative lack of interest (§§21 to 28).

are of no help towards morality when I've just been saying that there's no attaining morality without them. My answer would be this: there's no attaining morality without food either, but there's no connexion between morality and food. The fact that a ship can't begin to exist without the timbers of which it's built doesn't mean that the timbers are of 'help' to it. There's no reason for you to assume that, X being something without which Y could never have come about, Y came about as a result of the assistance of X. And indeed it can actually be argued that the attainment of wisdom is perfectly possible without the liberal studies; although moral values are things which have to be learnt, they are not learnt through these studies. Besides, what grounds could I possibly have for supposing that a person who has no acquaintance with books will never be a wise man? For wisdom does not lie in books. Wisdom publishes not words but truths – and I'm not sure that the memory isn't more reliable when it has no external aids to fall back on.

There is nothing small or cramped about wisdom. It is something calling for a lot of room to move. There are questions to be answered concerning physical as well as human matters, questions about the past and about the future, questions about things eternal and things ephemeral, questions about time itself. On this one subject of time just look how many questions there are. To start with, does it have an existence of its own? Next, does anything exist prior to time, independently of it? Did it begin with the universe, or did it exist even before then on the grounds that there was something in existence before the universe? There are countless questions about the soul alone – where it comes from, what its nature is, when it begins to exist, and how long it is in existence; whether it passes from one place to another, moving house, so to speak, on transfer to successive living creatures, taking on a different form with each, or is no more than once in service and is then released to roam the universe; whether it is a corporeal substance or not; what it will do when it ceases to act through us, how it will employ its freedom once it has escaped its cage here; whether it will forget its past and become conscious of its real nature from the actual moment of its parting from the body and departure for its new home on high. Whatever the field of physical or moral sciences you deal with, you will be given no rest by the mass of things to be learnt or investigated. And to enable matters of this range and scale to find unrestricted hospitality in our minds, everything superfluous must be turned out. Virtue will not bring herself to enter the limited space we offer her; something of great size requires plenty of room. Let everything else be evicted, and your heart completely opened to her.

'But it's a nice thing, surely, to be familiar with a lot of subjects.' Well, in that case let us retain just as much of them as we need. Would you consider a person open to criticism for putting superfluous objects on the same level as really useful ones by arranging on display in his house a whole array of costly articles, but not for cluttering himself up with a lot of superfluous furniture in the way of learning? To want to know more than is sufficient is a form of intemperance. Apart from which this kind of obsession with the liberal arts turns people into pedantic, irritating, tactless, self-satisfied bores, not learning what they need simply because they spend their time learning things they will never need. The scholar Didymus wrote four thousand works: I should feel sorry for him if he had merely read so many useless works. In these works he discusses such questions as Homer's origin, who was Aeneas' real mother, whether Anacreon's manner of life was more that of a lecher or that of a drunkard, whether Sappho slept with anyone who asked her, and other things that would be better unlearned if one actually knew them!

Don't you go and tell me now that life is long enough for this sort of thing! When you come to writers in our own school, for that matter, I'll show you plenty of works which could do with some ruthless pruning. It costs a person an enormous amount of time (and other people's ears an enormous amount of boredom) before he earns such compliments as 'What a learned person!' Let's be content with the much less fashionable label, 'What a good man!' . . .*

What about thinking how much time you lose through constantly being taken up with official matters, private matters or ordinary everyday matters, through sleep, through ill health? Measure your life: it just does not have room for so much.

I have been speaking about liberal studies. Yet look at the amount of useless and superfluous matter to be found in the philosophers. Even they have descended to the level of drawing distinctions between the uses of different syllables and discussing the proper meanings of prepositions and conjunctions. They have come to envy the philologist and the mathematician, and they have taken over all the inessential elements in those studies – with the result that they know more about devoting care and attention to their speech than about devoting such attention to their lives. Listen and let me show you the sorry consequences to which subtlety carried too far can lead, and what an enemy it is to truth. Protagoras declares that it is possible to argue either side of any question with equal force, even the question whether or not one can equally argue either side of any question! Nausiphanes declares that of the things which appear to us to exist, none exists any more than it does not exist. Parmenides declares that of all these phenomena none exists except the whole. Zeno of Elea has dismissed all such diffi-

* 15 lines (§§39 to 40, on further examples of worthless learning) are omitted.

culties by introducing another; he declares that nothing exists. The Pyrrhonean, Megarian, Eretrian and Academic schools pursue more or less similar lines; the last named have introduced a new branch of knowledge, non-knowledge.

Well, all these theories you should just toss on top of that heap of superfluous liberal studies. The people I first mentioned provide me with knowledge which is not going to be of any use to me, while the others snatch away from me any hopes of ever acquiring any knowledge at all. Superfluous knowledge would be preferable to no knowledge. One side offers me no guiding light to direct my vision towards the truth, while the other just gouges my eyes out. If I believe Protagoras there is nothing certain in the universe; if I believe Nausiphanes there is just the one certainty, that nothing is certain; if Parmenides, only one thing exists; if Zeno, not even one. Then what are we? The things that surround us, the things on which we live, what are they? Our whole universe is no more than a semblance of reality, perhaps a deceptive semblance, perhaps one without substance altogether. I should find it difficult to say which of these people annoy me most, those who would have us know nothing or the ones who refuse even to leave us the small satisfaction of knowing that we know nothing.

LETTER XC

WHO can doubt, my dear Lucilius, that life is the gift of the immortal gods, but that living well is the gift of philosophy? A corollary of this would be the certain conclusion that our debt to philosophy is greater than the debt we owe to the gods (by just so much as a good life is more of a blessing than, simply, life) had it not been for the fact that philosophy itself was something bestowed by the gods. They have given no one the present of a knowledge of philosophy, but everyone the means of acquiring it. For if they had made philosophy a blessing given to all and sundry, if we were born in a state of moral enlightenment, wisdom would have been deprived of the best thing about her – that she isn't one of the things which fortune either gives us or doesn't. As things are, there is about wisdom a nobility and magnificence in the fact that she doesn't just fall to a person's lot, that each man owes her to his own efforts, that one doesn't go to anyone other than oneself to find her. What would you have worth looking up to in philosophy if she were handed out free?

Philosophy has the single task of discovering the truth about the divine and human worlds. The religious conscience, the sense of duty, justice and all the rest of the close-knit, interdependent 'company of virtues', never leave her side. Philosophy has taught men to worship what is divine, to love what is human, telling us that with the gods belongs authority, and among human beings fellowship. That fellowship lasted for a long time intact, before men's greed broke society up – and impoverished even those she had brought most riches; for people cease to possess everything as soon as they want everything for themselves.

The first men on this earth, however, and their immediate descendants, followed nature unspoiled; they took a single person as their leader and their law, freely submitting to the decisions of an individual of superior merit. It is nature's way to subordinate the worse to the better. With dumb animals, indeed, the ones who dominate the group are either the biggest or the fiercest. The bull who leads the herd is not the weakling, but the one whose bulk and brawn has brought it victory over the other males. In a herd of elephants the tallest is the leader. Among human beings the highest merit means the highest position. So they used to choose their ruler

for his character. Hence peoples were supremely fortunate
when among them a man could never be more powerful than
others unless he was a better man than they were. For there is
nothing dangerous in a man's having as much power as he
likes if he takes the view that he has power to do only what
it is his duty to do.

In that age, then, which people commonly refer to as the
Golden Age, government, so Posidonius maintains, was in
the hands of the wise. They kept the peace, protected the
weaker from the stronger, urged and dissuaded, pointed out
what was advantageous and what was not. Their ability to
look ahead ensured that their peoples never went short of
anything, whilst their bravery averted dangers and their
devotedness brought well-being and prosperity to their
subjects. To govern was to serve, not to rule. No one used to
try out the extent of his power over those to whom he owed
that power in the first place. And no one had either reason or
inclination to perpetrate injustice, since people governing
well were equally well obeyed, and a king could issue no
greater threat to disobedient subjects than that of his own
abdication.

But with the gradual infiltration of the vices and the
resultant transformation of kingships into tyrannies, the need
arose for laws, laws which were themselves, to begin with,
drafted by the wise. Solon, who established Athens as a
democratic state, was one of the seven men of antiquity
celebrated for their wisdom. If the same age had produced
Lycurgus, an eighth name would have been added to that
revered number. The laws of Zaleucus and Charondas are
still admired. And it was not in public life or in the chambers
of lawyers that these two men learnt the constitutional
principles which they were to establish in Sicily (then in its
heyday) and throughout the Greek areas of Italy, but in the
secret retreat, now hallowed and famous, of Pythagoras.

Thus far I agree with Posidonius. But that philosophy discovered the techniques employed in everyday life, that I refuse to admit. I will not claim for philosophy a fame that belongs to technology. 'It was philosophy,' says Posidonius, 'that taught men how to raise buildings at a time when they were widely dispersed and their shelter consisted of huts or burrowed-out cliffs or hollowed tree trunks.' I for my part cannot believe that philosophy was responsible for the invention of these modern feats of engineering that rise up storey after storey, or the cities of today crowding one against the next, any more than of our fish-tanks, those enclosures designed to save men's gluttony from having to run the risk of storms and to ensure extravagance safe harbours of her own, however wildly the high seas may be raging, in which to fatten separately the different kinds of fish. Are you really going to tell me that philosophy taught the world to use keys and bolts on doors – which was surely nothing but a signal for greed? Was it philosophy that reared the towering buildings we know today, with all the danger they mean to the people living in them? It was not enough, presumably, for man to avail himself of whatever cover came to hand, to have found a shelter of some kind or other in nature without trouble and without the use of skills. Believe me, that age before there ever existed architects or builders was a happy age. The squaring off of timbers, the accurate cutting of beams with a saw that travels along a marked out line, all these things came in with extravagance.

The first of men with wedges split their wood.*

Yes, for they were not preparing a roof for a future banqueting-hall; and pines or firs were not continually being drawn through streets trembling at their passage on a long convoy

* Virgil, *Georgics*, I: 144.

of vehicles to support panelled ceilings heavy with gold.
Their huts were held up by a forked pole stood at either end,
and with close-packed branches and a sloping pile of leaves a
run-off was arranged for even heavy rains. This was the kind
of roof under which they lived and yet their lives were free
of care. For men in a state of freedom had thatch for their
shelter, while slavery dwells beneath marble and gold.

Another matter on which I disagree with Posidonius is
his belief that it was by wise men that tools were originally
invented. On that sort of basis there is nothing to stop him
saying that it was by philosophers that

> Discovered next were ways of snaring game,
> Of catching birds with lime, of setting dogs
> All round deep woods.*

It was human ingenuity, not wisdom, which discovered all
that. I disagree with him again where he maintains that it
was wise men who discovered iron and copper mining (when
the earth had been scorched by a forest fire and had melted to
produce a flow from surface veins of ore). The person who
discovers that sort of thing is the kind of person who makes it
his business to be interested in just that sort of thing. Nor, for
that matter, do I find it as nice a question as Posidonius does,
whether the hammer started to come into general use before
the tongs or the other way round. They were both invented
by some individual of an alert, perceptive turn of mind,
but not one with the qualities of greatness or of inspiration.
And the same applies to anything else the quest of which
involves a bent back and an earthward gaze.

The wise man then followed a simple way of life – which
is hardly surprising when you consider how even in this
modern age he seeks to be as little encumbered as he possibly

* Virgil, *Georgics*, I: 139–40.

can. How, I ask you, can you consistently admire both Daedalus and Diogenes? Tell me which of these two you would say was a wise man, the one who hit on the saw, or the one who on seeing a boy drinking water from the hollow of his hand, immediately took the cup out of his knapsack and smashed it, telling himself off for his stupidity in having superfluous luggage about him all that time, and curled himself up in a jar[56] and went to sleep. And today just tell me which of the following you consider the wiser man: the one who discovers a means of spraying saffron perfumes to a tremendous height from hidden pipes, who fills or empties channels in one sudden rush of water, who constructs a set of interchangeable ceilings for a dining room in such a way as to produce a constant succession of different patterns, with a change of ceiling at each course? Or the one who proves to others and to himself that nature makes no demand on us that is difficult or hard to meet and that we can live without the marble-worker and the engineer, that we can clothe ourselves without importing silks, that we can have the things we need for our ordinary purposes if we will only be content with what the earth has made available on its surface. If they only cared to listen to this man, the human race would realize that cooks are as unnecessary to them as are soldiers.

That race of men to whom taking care of the body was a straightforward enough matter were, if not philosophers, something very like it. The things that are essential are acquired with little bother; it is the luxuries that call for toil and effort. Follow nature and you will feel no need of craftsmen. It was nature's desire that we should not be kept occupied thus. She equipped us for everything she required us to contend with. 'But the naked body can't stand cold.' So what? Are the skins of wild beasts and other creatures not capable of giving us more than adequate protection against

the cold? Is it not a fact that many peoples make a covering
for their bodies out of bark, that feathers are sewn together
to serve as clothing, that even today the majority of the
Scythians wear the pelts of fox and mice, which are soft to
the touch and impervious to wind? Are you going to tell me
too that any people you care to mention never used their
hands to weave a basketwork of wattles, smear it all over with
common mud and then cover the whole roof with long grass-
stems and other material growing wild, and went through
winter weather, the rains streaming down the slopes of the
roof, without any worry? 'But we need some pretty dense
shade to keep off the heat of the sun in summer.' So what?
Have past ages not left us plenty of hiding places that have
been carved out by the ravages of time, or whatever other
cause one cares to suppose, and have developed into caves?
And again, is it not a fact that Syrtian tribes take shelter in
pits dug in the ground, as do other people who, because of
extreme sun temperatures, find nothing less than the baked
earth itself sufficiently substantial as a protective covering
against the heat? When nature granted all the other animals
a simple passage through life, she was not so unfair to man as
to make it impossible for him, for him alone, to live without
all these skills. Nature demanded nothing hard from us, and
nothing needs painful contriving to enable life to be kept
going. We were born into a world in which things were
ready to our hands; it is we who have made everything
difficult to come by through our own disdain for what is
easily come by. Shelter and apparel and the means of warming
body and food, all the things which nowadays entail tremendous trouble, were there for the taking, free to all, obtainable
at trifling effort. With everything the limit corresponded to
the need. It is we, and no one else, who have made those same
things costly, spectacular and obtainable only by means of a
large number of full-scale techniques.

Nature suffices for all she asks of us. Luxury has turned her back on nature, daily urging herself on and growing through all the centuries, pressing men's intelligence into the development of the vices. First she began to hanker after things that were inessential, and then after things that were injurious, and finally she handed the mind over to the body and commanded it to be the out and out slave of the body's whim and pleasure. All those trades that give rise to noise or hectic activity in the city are in business for the body, which was once in the position of the slave, having everything issued to it, and is now the master, having everything procured for it. This is the starting point for textile and engineering workshops, for the perfumes used by chefs, the sensual movements of our dancing teachers, even sensual and unmanly songs. And why? Because the bounds of nature, which set a limit to man's wants by relieving them only where there is necessity for such relief, have been lost sight of; to want simply what is enough nowadays suggests to people primitiveness and squalor.

It is incredible, Lucilius, how easily even great men can be carried away from the truth by the sheer pleasure of holding forth on a subject. Look at Posidonius, in my opinion one of those who have contributed most to philosophy, when he wants to give a description of how, in the first place, some threads are twisted and others drawn out from the soft, loose hank of wool, then how the warp has its threads stretched perpendicularly by means of hanging weights, and how the weft (worked in to soften the hard texture of the warp threads which compress it on either side) is made compact and close by means of the batten; he declares that philosophers invented the art of the weaver too, forgetting that philosophers had disappeared by the time this comparatively advanced type of weaving in which

> The warp is bound to the beam, and then its threads
> Are parted by the reed, the woof worked in
> Between with pointed shuttles and pressed home
> By the broad comb's fretted teeth*

had been evolved. He might have thought differently if he had only had the opportunity of seeing the looms of the present day, the end product of which is clothing which is not going to conceal a thing, clothing which is no help to modesty let alone the body! He then goes on to farmers, and gives an equally eloquent description of how the soil is broken up by the plough for the first time and then gone over again in order that the earth, thus loosened, may allow the roots more room to develop, and continues with the sowing of the seed and the lifting of the weeds to prevent any stray wild plants springing up and ruining the crop. All this, too, he represents as being the work of philosophers, as if agriculturists were not, now as ever, discovering plenty of new methods of increasing the soil's productivity.

Not content with these occupations, he proceeds to demean the philosopher to the bakery; he tells us how by imitating nature he began producing bread. 'The grain,' he says, 'is taken into the mouth and crushed by the coming together of the hard surfaces of the teeth; anything that escapes is carried back to the teeth again by the tongue, and the grain is finally mixed with saliva to enable it to pass down the lubricated throat with greater facility; on reaching the stomach, where it is cooked in an even heat, it is finally absorbed into the system. Taking this process as a model, someone or other placed one rough stone on top of another in imitation of the teeth, one set of which remains immobile and awaits the action of the other; the grains are then crushed by the friction of the one against the other, and are constantly re-subjected

* Ovid, *Metamorphoses*, VI:55 (apparently misquoted).

to it until they are reduced by this repeated grinding to a fine powder. He then sprinkled the resulting meal with water, and by going on manipulating it he made it plastic, and shaped it into the form of a loaf. This he first baked in a glowing hot earthenware vessel in hot ashes; later came the gradual discovery of ovens and other devices the heat of which is controllable at will.' Posidonius was not far off maintaining that the shoemaker's trade as well was invented by philosophers!

Now all these things were indeed discovered by the exercise of reason, but not by reason in its perfect form. They were invented by ordinary men, not by philosophers – just as, let me add, were the vessels we cross rivers and seas in, with sails designed to catch the drive of the winds and rudders at the stern to alter the vessel's course in this or that direction (the idea being taken from the fish, who steers with his tail, one slight movement of it to either side being enough to alter the direction of his darting course). 'All these things,' says Posidonius, 'were invented by our philosopher. They were, however, rather too unimportant for him to handle personally, and so he passed them over to the minions among his assistants.' No, the fact is that this sort of thing was not thought up by anyone other than the people who make them their concern today. We know very well that some have only appeared within living memory, the use, for example, of windows letting in the full daylight through transparent panes, or bathrooms heated from beneath with pipes set in the walls in order to diffuse the heat and thus maintain an even temperature at the highest as well as the lowest room levels. Need I mention the marble with which our temples and even houses are resplendent? Or the rounded and polished blocks on which we rest whole colonnades and buildings capable of holding large crowds of people? Or the shorthand symbols by means of which even a rapidly delivered speech is taken down and the hand is able to keep up with the quickness of the tongue? These are inventions of the lowest slaves. Philosophy is far above all this; she does not train men's hands: she is the instructress of men's minds.

You want to know, do you, what philosophy has unearthed, what philosophy has achieved? It is not the gracefulness of dance movements, nor the variety of sounds produced by horn or flute as they take in breath and transform it, in its passage through or out of the instrument, into notes. She does not set about constructing arms or walls or anything of use in war. On the contrary, her voice is for peace, calling all mankind to live in harmony. And she is not, I insist, the manufacturer of equipment for everyday essential purposes. Why must you make her responsible for such insignificant things? In her you see the mistress of the art of life itself. She has, indeed, authority over other arts, inasmuch as all activities that provide life with its apparatus must also be the servants of that of which life itself is the servant. Philosophy, however, takes as her aim the state of happiness. That is the direction in which she opens routes and guides us. She shows us what are real and what are only apparent evils. She strips men's minds of empty thinking, bestows a greatness that is solid and administers a check to greatness where it is puffed up and all an empty show; she sees that we are left in no doubt about the difference between what is great and what is bloated. And she imparts a knowledge of the whole of nature, as well as of herself. She explains what the gods are, and what they are like. . . .*

'Anacharsis,' says Posidonius, 'discovered the potter's wheel, the rotary motion of which shapes earthenware.' Then, mention of the potter's wheel being found in Homer,

* About 17 lines (§§28 to 30, in which Seneca appears to claim for philosophy complete and certain knowledge of the truth in religious or cosmological matters) have been omitted.

he would have us think that it is the passage in Homer, rather than his story, that is spurious. I maintain that Anacharsis was not responsible for this invention, and that even if he was, he discovered it as a philosopher, yes, but not in his capacity as a philosopher, in the same way as philosophers do plenty of things as men without doing them in their capacity as philosophers. Suppose, for example, a philosopher happens to be a very fast runner; in a race he will come first by virtue of his ability as a runner, not by virtue of his being a philosopher. I should like to show Posidonius some glass-blower moulding glass by means of his breath into a whole variety of shapes that could hardly be fashioned by the most careful hand – discoveries that have occurred in the period since the disappearance of the wise man. 'Democritus,' he says, 'is reported to be the discoverer of the arch, the idea of which is to bind a curving line of stones, set at slightly differing angles from each other, with a keystone.' This I should say was quite untrue. For there must have been both bridges and gateways before Democritus' time, and the upper parts of these generally have a curve to them. And it seems to have escaped your memory, Posidonius, that this same Democritus discovered a means of softening ivory, and a means of turning a pebble into an 'emerald' by boiling it, a method employed even today for colouring certain stones that man has discovered and found amenable to the process. These techniques may indeed have been discovered by a philosopher, but not in his capacity as a philosopher. For there are plenty of things which he does which one sees being done just as well if not with greater skill and dexterity by persons totally lacking in wisdom.

What has the philosopher investigated? What has the philosopher brought to light? In the first place, truth and nature (having, unlike the rest of the animal world, followed nature with more than just a pair of eyes, things slow to grasp divinity); and secondly, a rule of life, in which he has brought life into line with things universal. And he has taught us not just to recognize but to obey the gods, and to accept all that happens exactly as if it were an order from above. He has told us not to listen to false opinions, and has weighed and valued everything against standards which are true. He has condemned pleasures an inseparable element of which is subsequent regret, has commended the good things which will always satisfy, and for all to see has made the man who has no need of luck the luckiest man of all, and the man who is master of himself the master of all.

The philosophy I speak of is not the one* which takes the citizen out of public life and the gods out of the world we live in, and hands morality over to pleasure, but the philosophy which thinks nothing good unless it is honourable, which is incapable of being enticed astray by the rewards of men or fortune, and the very pricelessness of which lies in the fact that it cannot be bought at any price. And I do not believe that this philosophy was in existence in that primitive era in which technical skills were still unknown and useful knowledge was acquired through actual practical experience, or that it dates from an age that was happy, an age in which the bounties of nature were freely available for the use of all without discrimination, before avarice and luxury split human beings up and got them to abandon partnership for plunder. The men of that era were not philosophers, even if they acted as philosophers are supposed to act.† No other state of man could cause anyone greater admiration; if God were to allow a man to fashion the things of this earth and allot its peoples their social customs, that man would not be satisfied with any other system than the one which tradition says existed in those people's time, among whom

* Epicureanism.
† i.e. 'in accordance with nature'.

No farmers tilled ploughed fields; merely to mark
The line of boundaries dividing land
Between its owners was a sin; men shared
Their findings, and the earth herself then gave
All things more freely unsolicited.*

What race of men could be luckier? Share and share alike
they enjoyed nature. She saw to each and every man's
requirements for survival like a parent. What it all amounted
to was undisturbed possession of resources owned by the
community. I can surely call that race of men one of un-
paralleled riches, it being impossible to find a single pauper
in it.

Into this ideal state of things burst avarice, avarice which in
seeking to put aside some article or other and appropriate it
to its own use, only succeeded in making everything some-
body else's property and reducing its possessions to a fraction
of its previously unlimited wealth. Avarice brought in
poverty, by coveting a lot of possessions losing all that it had.
This is why although it may endeavour to make good its
losses, may acquire estate after estate by buying out or
forcing out its neighbours, enlarge country properties to the
dimensions of whole provinces, speak of 'owning some
property' when it can go on a long tour overseas without once
stepping off its own land, there is no extension of our
boundaries that can bring us back to our starting point.
When we have done everything within our power, we shall
possess a great deal: but we once possessed the world.

The earth herself, untilled, was more productive, her
yields being more than ample for the needs of peoples who
did not raid each other. With any of nature's products, men
found as much pleasure in showing others what they had discovered as they did in discovering it. No one could outdo or

* Virgil, *Georgics*, I: 125-8.

be outdone by any other. All was equally divided among
people living in complete harmony. The stronger had not
yet started laying hands on the weaker; the avaricious person
had not yet started hiding things away, to be hoarded for his
own private use, so shutting the next man off from actual
necessities of life; each cared as much about the other as
about himself. Weapons were unused; hands still unstained
with human blood had directed their hostility exclusively
against wild beasts.

Protected from the sun in some thick wood, living in
some very ordinary shelter under a covering of leaves pre-
serving them from the rigours of winter or the rain, those
people passed tranquil nights with never a sigh. We in our
crimson luxury toss and turn with worry, stabbed by needling
cares. What soft sleep the hard earth gave those people!
They had no carved or panelled ceilings hanging over
them. They lay out in the open, with the stars slipping past
above them and the firmament silently conveying onward
that mighty work of creation as it was carried headlong
below the horizon in the magnificent pageant of the night
sky. And they had clear views by day as well as by night of
this loveliest of mansions, enjoying the pleasure of watching
constellations falling away from the zenith and others rising
again from out of sight beneath the horizon. Surely it was a
joy to roam the earth with marvels scattered so widely
around one. You now, by contrast, go pale at every noise
your houses make, and if there is a creaking sound you run
away along your frescoed passages in alarm. Those people
had no mansions on the scale of towns. Fresh air and the
untrammelled breezes of the open spaces, the unoppressive
shade of a tree or rock, springs of crystal clarity, streams
which chose their own course, streams unsullied by the
work of man, by pipes or any other interference with their
natural channels, meadows whose beauty owed nothing to

man's art, that was the environment around their dwelling places in the countryside, dwelling places given a simple countryman's finish. This was a home in conformity with nature, a home in which one enjoyed living, and which occasioned neither fear of it nor fears for it, whereas nowa-days our own homes count for a large part of our feeling of insecurity.

But however wonderful and guileless the life they led, they were not wise men; this is a title that has come to be reserved for the highest of all achievements. All the same, I should be the last to deny that they were men of exalted spirit, only one step removed, so to speak, from the gods. There can be no doubt that before this earth was worn out it produced a better type of offspring. But though they all possessed a character more robust than that of today, and one with a greater aptitude for hard work, it is equally true that their personalities fell short of genuine perfection. For nature does not give a man virtue: the process of becoming a good man is an art. Certainly they did not go in search of gold or silver or the various crystalline stones to be found in the nethermost dregs of the earth. They were still merciful even to dumb animals. Man was far and away from killing man, not out of fear or provocation, but simply for entertain-ment. They had yet to wear embroidered clothing, and had yet to have gold woven into robes, or even mine it. But the fact remains that their innocence was due to ignorance and nothing else. And there is a world of difference between, on the one hand, choosing not to do what is wrong and, on the other, not knowing how to do it in the first place. They lacked the cardinal virtues of justice, moral insight, self-control and courage. There were corresponding qualities, in each case not unlike these, that had a place in their primi-tive lives; but virtue only comes to a character which has been thoroughly schooled and trained and brought to a pitch of perfection by unremitting practice. We are born for it, but not with it. And even in the best of people, until you cultivate it there is only the material for virtue, not virtue itself.

LETTER XCI

MY friend Liberalis is in some distress at the present moment following the news of the complete destruction of Lyons by fire. It is a disaster by which anyone might be shaken, let alone a person quite devoted to his home town. This event has left him groping for that staunchness of spirit which, naturally enough, he cultivated when it was a case of facing what to him were conceivable fears. One is not surprised, though, that there were never any advance fears of such an unexpected, virtually unheard of catastrophe, considering that there was no precedent for it. Plenty of cities have suffered damage by fire, but none has ever been blotted out by one. Even when its buildings have been set aflame by enemy hands, in many places the flames die out, and even if they are continually rekindled they are seldom so all-consuming as to leave nothing for tools to demolish. Earthquakes, too, have hardly ever been so ruinous and violent as to raze whole towns. There has never in fact been a fire so destructive as to leave nothing for a future fire to consume. But here a single night has laid low a host of architectural splendours any one of which might have been the glory of a separate city. In the depth of peace there has come such a blow as could not have been dreaded in war itself. Who would believe it? At a time when military conflict is in abeyance everywhere, when an international peace covers all parts of the globe, Lyons, the showpiece of Gaul, is lost to view. Fortune invariably allows those whom she strikes down in the sight of all a chance to fear what they were going to suffer. The fall of anything great generally takes time. But here a single night is all there was between a mighty city and no city at all. It was destroyed in fact in less time than I have taken telling you of its destruction.

Sturdy and resolute though he is when it comes to facing his own troubles, our Liberalis has been deeply shocked by the whole thing. And he has some reason to be shaken. What is quite unlooked for is more crushing in its effect, and unexpectedness adds to the weight of a disaster. The fact that it was unforeseen has never failed to intensify a person's grief. This is a reason for ensuring that nothing ever takes us by surprise. We should project our thoughts ahead of us at every turn and have in mind every possible eventuality instead of only the usual course of events. For what is there that fortune does not when she pleases fell at the height of its powers? What is there that is not the more assailed and buffeted by her the more lustrous its attraction? What is there that is troublesome or difficult for her? Her assaults do not always come along a single path, or even a well-recognized path. At one time she will call in the aid of our own hands in attacking us, at another she will be content with her own powers in devising for us dangers for which no one is responsible. No moment is exempt: in the midst of pleasures there are found the springs of suffering. In the middle of peace war rears its head, and the bulwarks of one's security are transformed into sources of alarm, friend turning foe and ally turning enemy. The summer's calm is upset by sudden storms more severe than those of winter. In the absence of any enemy we suffer all that an enemy might wreak on us. Overmuch prosperity if all else fails will hit on the instruments of its own destruction. Sickness assails those leading the most sensible lives, tuberculosis those with the strongest constitutions, retribution the utterly guiltless, violence the most secluded. Misfortune has a way of choosing some un-precedented means or other of impressing its power on those who might be said to have forgotten it. A single day strews in ruins all that was raised by a train of construction extend-ing over a long span of time and involving a great number of separate works and a great deal of favour on the part of heaven. To say a 'day', indeed, is to put too much of a brake on the calamities that hasten down upon us: an hour, an instant of time, suffices for the overthrow of empires. It would be some relief to our condition and our frailty if all things were as slow in their perishing as they were in their coming into being: but as it is, the growth of things is a tardy process and their undoing is a rapid matter.

Nothing is durable, whether for an individual or for a society; the destinies of men and cities alike sweep onwards. Terror strikes amid the most tranquil surroundings, and with-out any disturbance in the background to give rise to them calamities spring from the least expected quarter. States which stood firm through civil war as well as wars external collapse without a hand being raised against them. How few nations have made of their prosperity a lasting thing! This is why we need to envisage every possibility and to strengthen the spirit to deal with the things which may conceivably come about. Rehearse them in your mind: exile, torture, war, ship-wreck. Misfortune may snatch you away from your country, or your country away from you, may banish you into some wilderness – these very surroundings in which the masses suffocate may become a wilderness. All the terms of our human lot should be before our eyes; we should be anticipat-ing not merely all that commonly happens but all that is conceivably capable of happening, if we do not want to be overwhelmed and struck numb by rare events as if they were unprecedented ones; fortune needs envisaging in a thoroughly comprehensive way. Think how often towns in Asia or in Greece have fallen at a single earth tremor, how many villages in Syria or Macedonia have been engulfed, how often this form of disaster has wrought devastation in Cyprus, how often Paphos has tumbled about itself! Time and again we hear the news of the annihilation of a whole city, and how small a fraction of mankind are we who hear such news thus often! So let us face up to the blows of circumstance and be aware that whatever happens is never as serious as rumour makes it out to be.

So a city has burned, a wealthy city and the glory of the provinces of which it was a feature though it stood in a class of its own, perched as it was on a single hill and that not a hill of very great dimensions. But time will sweep away the very traces of every one of those cities of whose splendour and magnificence you nowadays hear. Look at the way the very foundations of once famous cities of Greece have been eroded by now to the point where nothing is left to show that they ever even existed. And it is not only the works of human hands that waste away, nor only structures raised by human skill and industry that the passing days demolish. Mountain massifs crumble away, whole regions have subsided, the waves have covered landmarks once far out of sight of the sea. The immense force of volcanic fires that once made the mountain-tops glow has eaten them away and reduced to lowly stature what once were soaring peaks, reassuring beacons to the mariner. The works of nature herself suffer. So it is only right that we should bear the overthrow of cities with resignation. They stand just to fall. Such is the sum total of the end that awaits them, whether it be the blast of a subterranean explosion throwing off the restraining weight above it, or the violence of floodwaters increasing to a prodigious degree underground until it breaks down everything in its way, or a volcanic outburst fracturing the earth's crust, or age (to which nothing is immune) overcoming them little by little, or plague carrying off its population and causing the deserted area to decay. It would be tedious to recount all the different ways by which fate may overtake them. One thing I know: all the works of mortal man lie under sentence of mortality; we live among things that are destined to perish.

Such, then, are the comforting reflections which I would offer our Liberalis, who burns with a kind of passion beyond belief for his birthplace – which it may be has only been consumed so as to be called to higher things. A setback has often cleared the way for greater prosperity. Many things have fallen only to rise to more exalted heights. That opponent of affluence in the capital, Timagenes, used to declare that the one reason fires distressed him was the knowledge that what would rise up afterwards would be of a better standard than what had burned. In the city of Lyons, too, one may presume that everyone will endeavour to make the work of restoration a greater, more noble achievement than what they have lost. May that work be of lasting duration, and may the new foundation be attended by happier auspices with a view to its lasting for a longer and indeed for all time! This is the hundredth year since the town came into being, and even for a human being such an age is by no means the uttermost limit. Founded by Plancus in an area of concentrated population, it owes its growth to its favourable situation: yet how many grievous blows it has had to suffer in the time it takes for a man to grow old.

So the spirit must be trained to a realization and an acceptance of its lot. It must come to see that there is nothing fortune will shrink from, that she wields the same authority over emperor and empire alike and the same power over cities as over men. There's no ground for resentment in all this. We've entered into a world in which these are the terms life is lived on – if you're satisfied with that, submit to them, if you're not, get out, whatever way you please. Resent a thing by all means if it represents an injustice decreed against yourself personally; but if this same constraint is binding on the lowest and the highest alike, then make your peace again with destiny, the destiny that unravels all ties. There's no justification for using our graves and all the variety of monuments we see bordering the highways as a measure of our stature. In the ashes all men are levelled. We're born unequal, we die equal. And my words apply as much to cities as to those who live in them. Ardea was taken, and so was Rome. The great lawgiver draws no distinctions between us according to our birth or the celebrity of our names, save only while we exist. On the reaching of mortality's end he declares, 'Away with snobbery; all that the earth carries shall forthwith be subject to one law without discrimination.' When it comes to all we're required to go through, we're equals. No one is more vulnerable than the next man, and no one can be more sure of his surviving to the morrow.

King Alexander of Macedon once took up the study of geometry – poor fellow, inasmuch as he would thus find out how minute the earth really was, the earth of which he had possessed himself of a tiny part; yes, 'poor fellow' I call him, for the reason that he was bound to discover that his title was a false one; for who can be 'Great' in an area of minute dimensions? Anyway, the points he was being instructed in were of some subtlety and such that the learning of them demanded the closest concentration, not the sort of thing that would be grasped by a crazed individual projecting his thoughts across the seas. 'Teach me,' he said, 'the easy things,' to which his instructor answered, 'These things are the same for everyone, equally difficult for all.' Well, imagine that nature is saying to you, 'Those things you grumble about are the same for everyone. I can give no one anything easier.

But anyone who likes may make them easier for himself.'
How? By viewing them with equanimity.

You must needs experience pain and hunger and thirst,
and grow old (assuming that you are vouchsafed a relatively
long stay among men) and be ill, and suffer loss, and finally
perish. But you needn't believe the chatter of the people
around you: there's nothing in all this that's evil, insupport-
able or even hard. Those people are afraid of these things by a
kind of general consent. Are you going to feel alarm at death,
then, in the same way as you might at some common report?
What could be more foolish than a man's being afraid of
people's words? My friend Demetrius has a nice way of
putting things when he says, as he commonly does, that to
him the utterances of the unenlightened are as noises emanat-
ing from the belly. 'What difference does it make to me,' he
asks, 'whether their rumblings come from their upper or
their nether regions?'

What utter foolishness it is to be afraid that those who have
a bad name can rob you of a good one. Just as the dread
aroused in you by some common report has proved ground-
less, so too is the dread of things of which you would never
be afraid if common report did not tell you to be. What
harm could ever come to a good man from being besmirched
by unwarranted gossip? We shouldn't even let it prejudice
us against death, which itself has an evil reputation. Yet none
of the people who malign it has put it to the test. Until one
does it's rather rash to condemn a thing one knows nothing
about. And yet one thing you do know and that is this, how
many people it's a blessing to, how many people it frees from
torture, want, maladies, suffering, weariness. And no one has
power over us when death is within our own power.

LETTER CIV

I HAVE got away to my place at Nomentum – getting away from what? Guess. The city? No, a fever. And just as it was infiltrating my defences, too. It had already taken a hold on me, my doctor being decided in his opinion that a disturbed, irregular pulse, its natural rhythm upset, was the start of it. Whereupon I immediately ordered my carriage out, and although my Paulina tried to hold me back, insisted on driving away. I kept saying the same thing as my mentor Gallio when he started sickening for a fever in Achaea. He immediately boarded a ship, assuring everyone that the disorder was to be put down to the place where he was living and not to his constitution.

I told Paulina this. She is forever urging me to take care of my health; and indeed as I come to realize the way her very being depends on mine, I am beginning, in my concern for her, to feel some concern for myself. So although old age has made me better at putting up with a lot of things, here I am coming to lose this advantage of being old. The notion occurs to me that inside this old frame there exists a young man as well and one is always less severe on a young man. The consequence is that since I haven't managed to get her to put a little more bravery into her love for me, she has managed to induce me to show a little more love and care for myself.

For concessions have to be made to legitimate emotions. There are times when, however pressing one's reasons to the contrary, one's dying breath requires to be summoned back and held back even as it is passing one's lips, even if this amounts to torture, simply out of consideration for one's dear ones. The good man should go on living as long as he ought to, not just as long as he likes. The man who does not value his wife or a friend highly enough to stay on a little longer in life, who persists in dying in spite of them, is a thoroughly self-indulgent character. This is a duty which the soul should also impose on itself when it is merely the convenience of near and dear ones that demands it. And not only if and when it feels the wish to die, but also if and when it has begun to carry out the wish, it should pause a while to fit in with their interests.

To return to life for another's sake is a sign of a noble spirit; it is something that great men have done on a number of occasions. Yet to give your old age greater care and attentiveness in the realization that this pleases any of the persons closest to you, or is in their interests, or would be likely to gratify them (and this in spite of the fact that the greatest reward of that period is the opportunity it gives you to adopt a relatively carefree attitude towards looking after yourself and a more adventurous manner of living), is also, to my mind, a mark of the highest possible kindness. Besides it brings you more than a little pleasure and recompense: for can anything be sweeter than to find that you are so dear to your wife that this makes you dearer to yourself? So it comes about that my Paulina succeeds in making me responsible for anxiety of my own as well as hers on my behalf.

I expect you're keen to hear what effect it had on my health, this decision of mine to leave? Well, no sooner had I left behind the oppressive atmosphere of the city and that reek of smoking cookers which pour out, along with a cloud of ashes, all the poisonous fumes they've accumulated in their interiors whenever they're started up, than I noticed the change in my condition at once. You can imagine how much stronger I felt after reaching my vineyards! I fairly waded into my food – talk about animals just turned out on to spring grass! So by now I am quite my old self again. That feeling of listlessness, being bodily ill at ease and mentally inefficient, didn't last. I'm beginning to get down to some whole-hearted work.

This is not something, however, to which mere surroundings are conducive, unless the mind is at its own disposal, able at will to provide its own seclusion even in crowded moments. On the contrary, the man who spends his time choosing one resort after another in a hunt for peace and quiet, will in every place he visits find something to prevent him from relaxing. The story is told that someone complained to Socrates that travelling abroad had never done him any good and received the reply: 'What else can you expect, seeing that you always take yourself along with you when you go abroad?' What a blessing it would be for some people if they could only lose themselves! As things are these persons are a worry and a burden, a source of demoralization and anxiety, to their own selves. What good does it do you to go overseas, to move from city to city? If you really want to escape the things that harass you, what you're needing is not to be in a different place but to be a different person. Suppose you've arrived in Athens, or suppose it's Rhodes – choose any country you like – what difference does the character of the place make? You'll only be importing your own with you. You'll still look on wealth as a thing to be valued: your poverty will be causing you torment, while (this being the most pathetic thing about it all) your poverty will be imaginary. However much you possess there's someone else who has more, and you'll be fancying yourself to be short of things you need to the exact extent to which you lag behind him. Another thing that you'll regard as something to be valued is success in public life; in which case you're going to feel resentment when so-and-so is elected consul (or when so-and-so is re-elected for that matter), and be jealous whenever you see a person's name appearing too often in the honours-lists. Your ambition will be running at so feverish a pitch that if anyone's ahead of you in the race you'll see yourself as coming last.

Death you'll think of as the worst of all bad things, though in fact there's nothing bad about it at all except the thing which comes before it – the fear of it. You'll be scared stiff by illusory as well as genuine dangers, haunted by imaginary alarms. What good will it do you to

> Have found a route past all those Argive forts
> And won escape right through the enemy's lines?*

Peace itself will supply you with new fears. If your mind has once experienced the shocks of fright you'll no longer have any confidence even in things which are perfectly safe; once it has acquired the habit of unthinking panic, it is incapable even of attending to its own self-preservation. For it runs away from dangers instead of taking steps to avert them, and we're far more exposed to them once our backs are turned.

To lose someone you love is something you'll regard as the hardest of all blows to bear, while all the time this will be as silly as crying because the leaves fall from the beautiful trees that add to the charm of your home. Preserve a sense of proportion in your attitude to everything that pleases you, and make the most of them while they are at their best. At one moment chance will carry off one of them, at another moment another; but the falling of the leaves is not difficult to bear, since they grow again, and it is no more hard to bear the loss of those whom you love and regard as brightening your existence; for even if they do not grow again they are replaced. 'But their successors will never be quite the same.' No, and neither will you. Every day, every hour sees a change in you, although the ravages of time are easier to see in others; in your own case they are far less obvious,

*Virgil, *Aeneid*, III:282–3.

because to you they do not show. While other people are snatched away from us, we are being filched away surreptitiously from ourselves.

Are you never going to give any of these considerations any thought and never going to apply any healing treatment to your wounds, instead of sowing the seeds of worry for yourself by hoping for this or that, or despairing of obtaining this or that other thing? If you're sensible you'll run the two together, and never hope without an element of despair, never despair without an element of hope.

What good has travel of itself ever been able to do anyone? It has never acted as a check on pleasure or a restraining influence on desires; it has never controlled the temper of an angry man or quelled the reckless impulses of a lover; never in fact has it rid the personality of a fault. It has not granted us the gift of judgement, it has not put an end to mistaken attitudes. All it has ever done is distract us for a little while, through the novelty of our surroundings, like children fascinated by something they haven't come across before. The instability, moreover, of a mind which is seriously unwell, is aggravated by it, the motion itself increasing the fitfulness and restlessness. This explains why people, after setting out for a place with the greatest of enthusiasm, are often more enthusiastic about getting away from it; like migrant birds, they fly on, away even quicker than they came.

Travel will give you a knowledge of other countries, it will show you mountains whose outlines are quite new to you, stretches of unfamiliar plains, valleys watered by perennial streams; it will allow you to observe the unique features of this or that river, the way in which, for example, the Nile rises in summer flood, or the Tigris vanishes from sight and at the completion of its journey through hidden subterranean regions is restored to view with its volume undiminished, or the way the Meander, theme of every poet's early training exercises, winds about, loop after loop, and again and again is carried close to its own bed and then once more diverted into a different course before it can flow into its own stream. But travel won't make a better or saner man of you. For this we must spend time in study and in the writings of wise men, to learn the truths that have emerged from their researches, and carry on the search ourselves for the answers that have not yet been discovered. This is the way to liberate the spirit that still needs to be rescued from its miserable state of slavery.

So long, in fact, as you remain in ignorance of what to aim at and what to avoid, what is essential and what is superfluous, what is upright or honourable conduct and what is not, it will not be travelling but drifting. All this hurrying from place to place won't bring you any relief, for you're travelling in the company of your own emotions, followed by your troubles all the way. If only they were really following you! They'd be farther away from you: as it is they're not at your back, but on it! That's why they weigh you down with just the same uncomfortable chafing wherever you are. It's medicine, not a particular part of the world, that a person needs if he's ill. Suppose someone has broken his leg or dislocated a joint; he doesn't get into a carriage or board a ship: he calls in a doctor to have the fracture set or the dislocation reduced. Well then, when a person's spirit is wrenched or broken at so many points, do you imagine that it can be put right by a change of scenery, that that sort of trouble isn't so serious that it can't be cured by an outing?

Travelling doesn't make a man a doctor or a public speaker: there isn't a single art which is acquired merely by being in one place rather than another. Can wisdom, then, the greatest art of all, be picked up in the course of taking a trip? Take my word for it, the trip doesn't exist that can set you beyond the reach of cravings, fits of temper, or fears.

If it did, the human race would be off there in a body. So long as you carry the sources of your troubles about with you, those troubles will continue to harass and plague you wherever you wander on land or on sea. Does it surprise you that running away doesn't do you any good? The things you're running away from are with you all the time.

What you must do, then, is mend your ways and get rid of the burden you're carrying. Keep your cravings within safe limits. Scour every trace of evil from your personality. If you want to enjoy your travel, you must make your travelling companion a healthy one. So long as you associate with a person who's mean and grasping you will remain a money-minded individual yourself. So long as you keep arrogant company, just so long will conceit stick to you. Cruelty you'll never say goodbye to while you share the same roof with a torturer. Familiarity with adulterers will only inflame your desires. If you wish to be stripped of your vices you must get right away from the examples others set of them. The miser, the swindler, the bully, the cheat, who would do you a lot of harm by simply being near you, are actually inside you. Move to better company: live with the Catos, with Laelius, with Tubero. If you like Greek company too, attach yourself to Socrates and Zeno: the one would teach you how to die should it be forced upon you, the other how to die before it is forced upon you. Live with Chrysippus, live with Posidonius; they will give you a knowledge of man and the universe; they will tell you to be a practical philosopher: not just to entertain your listeners to a clever display of language, but to steel your spirit and brace it against whatever threatens. For the only safe harbour in this life's tossing, troubled sea is to refuse to be bothered about what the future will bring and to stand ready and confident, squaring the breast to take without skulking or flinching whatever fortune hurls at us.

When she created us, nature endowed us with noble aspirations, and just as she gave certain animals ferocity, others timidity, others cunning, so to us she gave a spirit of exalted ambition, a spirit that takes us in search of a life of, not the greatest safety, but the greatest honour – a spirit very like the universe, which, so far as mortal footsteps may, it follows and adopts as a model. It is self-assertive; it feels assured of honour and respect; it is master of all things; it is above all things; it should accordingly give in to nothing; in nothing should it see a burden calculated to bow the shoulders of a man.

> Shapes frightening to the sight, Hardship and Death*

are not so at all if one can break through the surrounding darkness and look directly at them. Many are the things that have caused terror during the night and been turned into matters of laughter with the coming of daylight.

> Shapes frightening to the sight, Hardship and Death.

Our Virgil perfectly rightly says that they are frightening, not in reality, but 'to the sight', in other words that they seem so but in fact are not. Just what is there about them that is as terrifying as legend would have us believe? Why, Lucilius, I ask you why should any real man be afraid of hardship, or any human being be afraid of death? I constantly meet people who think that what they themselves can't do can't be done, who say that to bear up under the things we Stoics speak of is beyond the capacity of human nature. How much more highly I rate these people's abilities than they do themselves! I say that they are just as capable as others of doing these things, but won't. In any event what person actually trying them has found them prove beyond him? Who hasn't

* Virgil, *Aeneid*, VI:277.

noticed how much easier they are in the actual doing? It's not because they're hard that we lose confidence; they're hard because we lack the confidence.

If you still need an example, take Socrates, an old man who had known his full share of suffering, who had taken every blow life could inflict, and still remained unbeaten either by poverty, a burden for him aggravated by domestic worries, or by constant hardships, including those endured on military service. Apart from what he had to contend with at home – whether one thinks of his wife with her shrewish ways and nagging tongue, or his intractable children, more like their mother than their father – his whole life was lived either in war-time or under tyranny or under a 'democracy' that outdid even wars and tyrants in its cruelties. The war went on for twenty-seven years. After the fighting was ended, the state was handed over to the mercy of the Thirty Tyrants, a considerable number of whom were hostile to him. The final blow was his conviction and sentence on the most serious of charges: he was accused of blasphemy and of corrupting the younger generation, whom, it was alleged, he turned into rebels against God, their fathers and the state. After that came the prison and the poison. And so little effect did all this have on Socrates' spirit, it did not even affect the expression on his face. What a rare and wonderful story of achievement! To the very last no one ever saw Socrates in any particular mood of gaiety or depression. Through all the ups and downs of fortune his was a level temperament.

Would you like another example? Take the modern one of Marcus Cato, with whom fortune dealt in an even more belligerent and unremitting fashion. At every point she stood in his way, even at the end, at his death; yet he demonstrated that a brave man can live in defiance of fortune and can die in defiance of fortune. The whole of his life was passed either in civil war or in conditions of developing civil conflict. And of him no less than of Socrates it is possible to say that he carried himself clear of slavery* (unless, perhaps, you take the view that Pompey, Caesar and Crassus were friends of freedom). When his country was in a state of constant change, no one ever saw a change in Cato. In every situation he was placed in, he showed himself always the same man, whether in office as praetor, in defeat at the polls, under attack in court, as governor in his province, on the public platform, in the field, or in death itself. In that moment, too, of panic for the Republic, when Caesar stood on the one side, backed by ten legions of the finest fighting men and the entire resources and support of foreign countries as well, and on the other stood Pompey, by himself a match for all comers, and when people were moving to join either the one or the other, Cato all on his own established something of a party pledged to fight for the Republic. If you try to picture the period to yourself you will see on the one side the populace, the mob all agog for revolution, on the other the time-honoured elect of Rome, the aristocracy and knighthood; and two forlorn figures, Cato and republicanism, between them. You will find it an impressive sight, I can assure you, as you watch

> The Son of Atreus and King Priam with
> Achilles wroth with both.†

For there is Cato denouncing each of them, trying to disarm the pair of them. And the way he casts his vote between them is: 'If Caesar wins, I kill myself; if Pompey, I go into exile.' What had a man to fear who, win or lose, had dictated to himself such a choice of fates as might have been decreed him by an utterly exasperated enemy? And that is how he came to die, carrying out his own self-sentence.

* At this point of uncertainty in the text I have adopted the reading *servituti se eduxisse* suggested by Haase.

† Virgil, *Aeneid*, I:458.

You will see, too, the capacity of man for hardship: on foot at the head of his troops he crossed the deserts of North Africa. You see that thirst can be endured as well: always in armour, trailing over a sun-baked plateau the remnants of a beaten army, an army without supplies, he was invariably the last to drink whenever they came upon water. You see that a man can think equally little of either the distinction of office or the stigma of rejection: on the day of his election defeat he played fives at the place of polling. You see that men can defy the might of their superiors: for, with no one daring offend either Caesar or Pompey except to curry favour with the other, Cato challenged the pair of them simultaneously. You see that a man can think as little of death as of exile: he condemned himself to both, and war in the meantime.

We, then, can show as spirited an attitude to just the same things if we will only choose to slip the yoke from our necks. But first we have to reject the life of pleasures; they make us soft and womanish; they are insistent in their demands, and what is more, require us to make insistent demands on fortune. And then we need to look down on wealth, which is the wage of slavery. Gold and silver and everything else that clutters our prosperous homes should be discarded. Freedom cannot be won without sacrifice. If you set a high value on her, everything else must be valued at little.

LETTER CV

YES, I'll give you some rules to observe that will enable you to live in greater safety. You for your part I suggest should listen as carefully to the advice I give you as you would if I were advising you on how to look after your health at Ardea.

Now think of the things which goad man into destroying man: you'll find that they are hope, envy, hatred, fear and contempt. Contempt is the least important of the lot, so much so that a number of men have actually taken shelter behind it for protection's sake. For if a person feels contempt for someone, he tramples on him, doubtless, but he passes on. No one pursues an unremitting and persistent policy of injury to a man for whom he feels nothing but contempt. Even in battle the man on the ground is left alone, the fighting being with those still on their feet. Coming to hope, so long as you own nothing likely to arouse the greed or grasping instincts of others, so long as you possess nothing out of the ordinary (for people covet even the smallest things if they are rare or little known),* you'll have nothing to worry about from the hopes of grasping characters. Envy you'll escape if you haven't obtruded yourself on other people's notice, if you haven't flaunted your possessions, if you've learnt to keep your satisfaction to yourself. Hatred either comes from giving offence, and that you'll avoid by refraining from deliberately provoking anyone, or is quite uncalled for: here your safeguard will be ordinary tact. It is a kind of hatred that has been a source of danger to a lot of people; men have been hated without having any actual enemy. As regards not being feared, a moderate fortune and an easy-going nature will secure you that. People should see that you're not a person it is dangerous to offend: and with you a reconciliation should be both easy and dependable. To be feared inside your own home, it may be added, is as much a source of trouble as being feared outside it – slave or free, there isn't a man who hasn't power enough to do you injury. Besides, to be feared is to fear: no one has been able to strike terror into others and at the same time enjoy peace of mind himself. There remains contempt.

* The text at this point is corrupt. I have adopted the emendations *si parum nota* and *si rara* suggested by Buecheler and Madvig.

The person who has made contempt his ally, who has been despised because he has chosen to be despised, has the measure of it under his control. Its disadvantages are negatived by the possession of respected qualities and of friends having influence with some person with the necessary influence. Such influential friends are people with whom it is well worth having ties, without being so tied up with them that their protection costs you more than the original danger might have done.

But nothing will help quite so much as just keeping quiet, talking with other people as little as possible, with yourself as much as possible. For conversation has a kind of charm about it, an insinuating and insidious something that elicits secrets from us just like love or liquor. Nobody will keep the things he hears to himself, and nobody will repeat just what he hears and no more. Neither will anyone who has failed to keep a story to himself keep the name of his informant to himself. Every person without exception has someone to whom he confides everything that is confided to himself. Even supposing he puts some guard on his garrulous tongue and is content with a single pair of ears, he will be the creator of a host of later listeners – such is the way in which what was but a little while before a secret becomes common rumour.

Never to wrong others takes one a long way towards peace of mind. People who know no self-restraint lead stormy and disordered lives, passing their time in a state of fear commensurate with the injuries they do to others, never able to relax. After every act they tremble, paralysed, their consciences continually demanding an answer, not allowing them to get on with other things. To expect punishment is to suffer it; and to earn it is to expect it. Where there is a bad conscience, some circumstance or other may provide one with impunity, but never with freedom from anxiety; for a person takes the attitude that even if he isn't found out, there's always the possibility of it. His sleep is troubled. Whenever he talks about someone else's misdeed he thinks of his own, which seems to him all too inadequately hidden, all too inadequately blotted out of people's memories. A guilty person sometimes has the luck to escape detection, but never to feel sure of it.

LETTER CVII

WHERE's that moral insight of yours? Where's that acuteness of perception? Or magnanimity? Does something as trivial as that upset you? Your slaves have seen your absorption in business as their chance to run away. So be it, you have been let down by friends – for by all means let them keep the name we mistakenly bestowed on them and be called such just to heighten their disgrace; but the fact is that your affairs have been freed for good and all of a number of people on whom all your trouble was being wasted and who considered you insufferable to anyone but yourself. There's nothing unusual or surprising about it all. To be put out by this sort of thing is as ridiculous as grumbling about being spattered in the street or getting dirty where it's muddy. One has to accept life on the same terms as the public baths, or crowds, or travel. Things will get thrown at you and things will hit you. Life's no soft affair. It's a long road you've started on: you can't but expect to have slips and knocks and falls, and get tired, and openly wish – a lie – for death. At one place you will part from a companion, at another bury one, and be afraid of one at another. These are the kind of things you'll come up against all along this rugged journey. Wanting to die? Let the personality be made ready to face everything; let it be made to realize that it has come to terrain on which thunder and lightning play, terrain on which

> Grief and vengeful Care have set their couch,
> And pallid Sickness dwells, and drear Old Age.*

This is the company in which you must live out your days. Escape them you cannot, scorn them you can. And scorn them you will if by constant reflection you have anticipated future happenings. Everyone faces up more bravely to a thing for which he has long prepared himself, sufferings, even, being withstood if they have been trained for in advance. Those who are unprepared, on the other hand, are panic-stricken by the most insignificant happenings. We must see to it that nothing takes us by surprise. And since it is invariably unfamiliarity that makes a thing more formidable than it really is, this habit of continual reflection will ensure that no form of adversity finds you a complete beginner.

'I've been deserted by my slaves!' Others have been plundered, incriminated, set upon, betrayed, beaten up, attacked with poison or with calumny – mention anything you like, it has happened to plenty of people. A vast variety of missiles are launched with us as their target. Some are planted in our flesh already, some are hurtling towards us at this very moment, others merely grazing us in passing on their way to other targets. Let's not be taken aback by any of the things we're born to, things no one need complain at for the simple reason that they're the same for everybody. Yes, the same for everybody; for even if a man does escape something, it was a thing which he might have suffered. The fairness of a law does not consist in its effect being actually felt by all alike, but in its having been laid down for all alike. Let's get this sense of justice firmly into our heads and pay up without

* Virgil, *Aeneid*, VI:274-5.

grumbling the taxes arising from our mortal state. Winter brings in the cold, and we have to shiver; summer brings back the heat and we have to swelter. Bad weather tries the health and we have to be ill. Somewhere or other we are going to have encounters with wild beasts, and with man, too, – more dangerous than all those beasts. Floods will rob us of one thing, fire of another. These are conditions of our existence which we cannot change. What we can do is adopt a noble spirit, such a spirit as befits a good man, so that we may bear up bravely under all that fortune sends us and bring our wills into tune with nature's; reversals, after all, are the means by which nature regulates this visible realm of hers: clear skies follow cloudy; after the calm comes the storm; the winds take turns to blow; day succeeds night; while part of the heavens is in the ascendant, another is sinking. It is by means of opposites that eternity endures.

This is the law to which our minds are needing to be reconciled. This is the law they should be following and obeying. They should assume that whatever happens was bound to happen and refrain from railing at nature. One can do nothing better than endure what cannot be cured and attend uncomplainingly the God at whose instance all things come about. It is a poor soldier that follows his commander grumbling. So let us receive our orders readily and cheerfully, and not desert the ranks along the march – the march of this glorious fabric of creation in which everything we shall suffer is a strand. And let us address Jupiter, whose guiding hand directs this mighty work, in the way our own Cleanthes did, in some most expressive lines which I may perhaps be pardoned for translating in view of the example set here by that master of expressiveness, Cicero. If you like them, so much the better; if not, you will at least know that I was following Cicero's example.

Lead me, Master of the soaring vault
Of Heaven, lead me, Father, where you will.
I stand here prompt and eager to obey.
And ev'n suppose I were unwilling, still
I should attend you and know suffering,
Dishonourably and grumbling, when I might
Have done so and been good as well. For Fate
The willing leads, the unwilling drags along.*

Let us speak and live like that. Let fate find us ready and
eager. Here is your noble spirit – the one which has put itself
in the hands of fate; on the other side we have the puny
degenerate spirit which struggles, and which sees nothing
right in the way the universe is ordered, and would rather
reform the gods than reform itself.

LETTER CVIII

THE subject you ask me about is one of those in which
knowledge has no other justification than the knowledge itself. Nevertheless, and just because it is so justified, you're in a
great hurry and reluctant to wait for the encyclopedia of
ethics I'm compiling at this very moment. Well, I shall let
you have your answer immediately, but first I'm going to
tell you how this enthusiasm for learning, with which I can
see you're on fire, is to be brought under control if it isn't
going to stand in its own way. What is wanted is neither
haphazard dipping nor a greedy onslaught on knowledge in
the mass. The whole will be reached through its parts, and

* St Augustine quotes this fragment of Cleanthes as Seneca's (*De
Civitate Dei*, V:8).

the burden must be adjusted to our strength. We mustn't take on more than we can manage. You shouldn't attempt to absorb all you want to – just what you've room for; simply adopt the right approach and you will end up with room for all you want. The more the mind takes in the more it expands.

I remember a piece of advice which Attalus gave me in the days when I practically laid siege to his lecture hall, always first to arrive and last to go, and would draw him into a discussion of some point or other even when he was out taking a walk, for he was always readily available to his students, not just accessible. 'A person teaching and a person learning,' he said, 'should have the same end in view: the improvement of the latter.' A person who goes to a philosopher should carry away with him something or other of value every day; he should return home a sounder man or at least more capable of becoming one. And he will: for the power of philosophy is such that she helps not only those who devote themselves to her but also those who come into contact with her. A person going out into the sun, whether or not this is what he is going out for, will acquire a tan. Customers who sit around rather too long in a shop selling perfumes carry the scent of the place away with them. And people who have been with a philosopher are bound to have derived from it something of benefit even to the inattentive. Note that I say the inattentive, not the hostile.

'That's all very well, but don't we all know certain people who have sat at a philosopher's feet year after year without acquiring even a semblance of wisdom?' Of course I do – persevering, conscientious people, too. I prefer to call them a philosopher's squatters, not students. Some come not to learn but just to hear him, in the same way as we're drawn to a theatre, for the sake of entertainment, to treat our ears to a play, or music, or an address. You'll find that a large proportion of the philosopher's audience is made up of this element, which regards his lecture-hall as a place of lodging for periods of leisure. They're not concerned to rid themselves of any faults there, or acquire any rule of life by which to test their characters, but simply to enjoy to the full the pleasures the ear has to offer. Admittedly some of them actually come with notebooks, but with a view to recording not the content of the lecture, but words from it – to be passed on to others with the same lack of profit to the hearer as they themselves derived from hearing them. Some of them are stirred by the noble sentiments they hear; their faces and spirits light up and they enter into the emotions of the speaker, going into a transport just like the eunuch priests who work themselves into a frenzy, to order, at the sound of a Phrygian flute. They are captivated and aroused not by a din of empty words, but by the splendour of the actual content of the speaker's words – any expression of bold or spirited defiance of death or fortune making you keen to translate what you've heard into action straight away. They are deeply affected by the words and become the persons they are told to be – or would if the impression on their minds were to last, if this magnificent enthusiasm were not immediately intercepted by that discourager of noble conduct, the crowd: very few succeed in getting home in the same frame of mind.

It is easy enough to arouse in a listener a desire for what is honourable; for in every one of us nature has laid the foundations or sown the seeds of the virtues. We are born to them all, all of us, and when a person comes along with the necessary stimulus, then those qualities of the personality are awakened, so to speak, from their slumber. Haven't you noticed how the theatre murmurs agreement whenever something is spoken the truth of which we generally recognize and unanimously confirm?

The poor lack much, the greedy everything.

The greedy man does no one any good,
But harms no person more than his own self.*

Your worst miser will clap these lines and be delighted at
hearing his own faults lashed in this manner. Imagine how
much more likely it is that this will happen when such things
are being said by a philosopher, interspersing passages of sound
advice with lines of poetry calculated to deepen their hold on
unenlightened minds. For 'the constricting requirements of
verse,' as Cleanthes used to say, 'give one's meaning all the
greater force, in the same way as one's breath produces a far
greater noise when it is channelled through a trumpet's
long and narrow tube before its final expulsion through the
widening opening at the end.' The same things stated in
prose are listened to with less attention and have much less
impact. When a rhythm is introduced, when a fine idea is
compressed into a definite metre, the very same thought
comes hurtling at one like a missile launched from a fully
extended arm. A lot, for example, is said about despising
money. The listener is told at very considerable length that
men should look on riches as consisting in the spirit and not in
inherited estates, and that a man is wealthy if he has attuned
himself to his restricted means and has made himself rich on
little. But verses such as the following he finds a good deal
more striking.

He needs but little who desires but little.

He has his wish, whose wish can be
To have what is enough.

When we hear these lines and others like them, we feel
impelled to admit the truth. The people for whom nothing

* Both quotations, and the next two, are believed to be fragments of
plays of Publilius Syrus.

is ever enough admire and applaud such a verse and publicly
declare their distaste for money. When you see them in such
a mood, keep at them and drive this home, piling it on them,
having nothing to do with plays on words, syllogisms,
sophistries and all the other toys of sterile intellectual clever-
ness. Speak out against the love of money. Speak out against
extravagance. When you see that you've achieved something
and had an effect on your listeners, lay on all the harder. It is
hardly believable how much can be achieved by this sort of
speech, aimed at curing people, wholly directed to the good
of the people listening. When the character is impressionable
it is easily won over to a passion for what is noble and honourable; while a person's character is still malleable, and only
corrupted to a mild degree, truth strikes deep if she finds the
right kind of advocate.

For my part, at any rate, when I heard Attalus winding up
the case against the faults of character, the mistaken attitudes
and the evils generally of the lives we lead, I frequently felt a
sense of the sorry plight of the human race and looked on him
as a kind of sublime being who had risen higher than the
limits of human aspiration. He himself would use the Stoic
term 'king' of himself; but to me he seemed more than a
king, as being a man who had the right to pass judgement on
the conduct and the character of monarchs. And when he
began extolling to us the virtues of poverty and showing us
how everything which went beyond our actual needs was
just so much unnecessary weight, a burden to the man who
had to carry it, I often had a longing to walk out of that lecture
hall a poor man. When he started exposing our pleasures and
commending to us, along with moderation in our diet,
physical purity and a mind equally uncontaminated, uncontaminated not only by illicit pleasures but by unnecessary
ones as well, I would become enthusiastic about keeping the
appetites for food and drink firmly in their place. With the

result that some of this, Lucilius, has lasted with me right through life. For I started out on it all with tremendous energy and enthusiasm, and later, after my return to public life, I managed to retain a few of the principles as regards which I had made this promising beginning. This is how I came to give up oysters and mushrooms for the rest of my life (for they are not really food to us but titbits which induce people who have already had as much as they can take to go on eating – the object most desired by gluttons and others who stuff themselves with more than they can hold – being items which will come up again as easily as they go down). This too is why throughout life I have always abstained from using scent, as the best smell a body can have is no smell at all. This is why no wine ever finds its way into my stomach. This is the reason for my life-long avoidance of hot baths, believing as I do that it is effeminate as well as pointless to stew one's body and exhaust it with continual sweating. Some other things to which I once said good-bye have made their reappearance, but nevertheless, in these cases in which I have ceased to practise total abstinence, I succeed in observing a limit, which is something hardly more than a step removed from total abstinence (and even perhaps more difficult – with some things less effort of will is required to cut them out altogether than to have recourse to them in moderation).

Now that I've started disclosing to you how much greater my enthusiasm was in taking up philosophy as a young man than it is when it comes to keeping it up in my old age, I shan't be ashamed to confess the passionate feelings which Pythagoras inspired in me. Sotion used to tell us why Pythagoras, and later Sextius, was a vegetarian. Each had a quite different reason, but each was a striking one. Sextius believed that man had enough food to sustain him without shedding blood, and that when men took this tearing of flesh so far that it became a pleasure a habit of cruelty was formed. He argued in addition that the scope for people's extravagance was in any case something that should be reduced; and he gave reasons for inferring that variety of diet was incompatible with our physical make-up and inimical to health. Pythagoras, on the other hand, maintained that all creatures were inter-related and that there was a system of exchange of souls involving transmigration from one bodily form to another. If we are to believe Pythagoras, no soul ever undergoes death, or even a suspension of its existence except perhaps for the actual moment of transfusion into another body. This is not the moment for inquiring by what stages or at what point a soul completes its wanderings through a succession of other habitations and reverts to human form. It is enough for our present purposes that he has instilled into people a dread of committing the crime of parricide, in view of the possibility that they might, all unknowing, come across the soul of an ancestor and with knife or teeth do it dreadful outrage, assuming that the spirit of a relative might be lodging in the flesh concerned. After setting out this theory and supplementing it with arguments of his own, Sotion would say, 'You cannot accept the idea of souls being assigned to one body after another, and the notion that what we call death is only a move to another home? You cannot accept that the soul which was once that of a man may sojourn in wild beasts, or in our own domestic animals, or in the creatures of the deep? You cannot accept that nothing ever perishes on this earth, instead merely undergoing a change in its whereabouts? And that the animal world, not just the heavenly bodies that revolve in their unalterable tracks, moves in cycles, with its souls propelled along an orbital path of their own? Well, the fact that these ideas are ones which have been accepted by great men should make you suspend judgement. You should preserve an open mind on the whole subject anyway. For if these ideas are correct, to

abstain from eating the flesh of animals will mean guiltless-
ness; and even if they are not, it will still mean frugal living.
What do you lose by believing in it all? All I am depriving
you of is what the lions and the vultures feed on.'

Fired by this teaching I became a vegetarian, and by the
time a year had gone by was finding it an enjoyable as well
as an easy habit. I was beginning to feel that my mind was
more active as a result of it – though I would not take my
oath to you now that it really was. I suppose you want to
know how I came to give up the practice. Well, my years
as a young man coincided with the early part of Tiberius'
reign, when certain religious cults of foreign origin were
being promoted, and among other things abstinence from
certain kinds of animal food was regarded as evidence of
adherence to such superstitions. So at the request of my father,
who did not really fear my being prosecuted, but who
detested philosophy, I resumed my normal habits. And in
fact he had little difficulty in persuading me to adopt a fuller
diet. Another thing, though, which Attalus used to recommend was a hard mattress; and that is the kind I still use even
in my old age, the kind which shows no trace of a body
having slept on it. I tell you all this just to show you the
tremendous enthusiasm with which the merest beginner will
set about attaining the very highest goals provided someone
gives him the necessary prompting and encouragement.
Things tend, in fact, to go wrong; part of the blame lies on
the teachers of philosophy, who today teach us how to argue
instead of how to live, part on their students, who come to
the teachers in the first place with a view to developing not
their character but their intellect. The result has been the
transformation of philosophy, the study of wisdom, into
philology, the study of words.

The object which we have in view, after all, makes a
great deal of difference to the manner in which we approach

any subject. If he intends to become a literary scholar, a person examining his Virgil does not say to himself when he reads that magnificent phrase

> Irrestorable, Time flies*

'We need to bestir ourselves; life will leave us behind unless we make haste; the days are fleeting by, carried away at a gallop, carrying us with them; we fail to realize the pace at which we are being swept along; here we are making comprehensive plans for the future and generally behaving as if we had all the leisure in the world when there are precipices all around us.' No, his purpose is to note that Virgil invariably uses this word 'flies' whenever he speaks of the swift passage of time.

> Life's finest days, for us poor human beings,
> Fly first; the sicknesses and sufferings,
> A bleak old age, the snatching hand
> Implacable of merciless death, creep near.†

It is the person with philosophy in his mind who takes these words in the way they are meant to be taken. 'Virgil,' he says, 'never speaks of the hours as "passing" but as "flying", this being the swiftest form of travel. He is also telling us that the finest ones are the first to be borne away. Then why are we so slow to get ourselves moving so as to be able to keep up with the pace of this swiftest of all things?' The best parts of life are flitting by, the worse are to come. The wine which is poured out first is the purest wine in the bottle, the heaviest particles and any cloudiness settling to the bottom. It is just the same with human life. The best comes first. Are we going to let others drain it so as to keep the dregs for ourselves? Let that sentence stick in your mind, accepted as unquestioningly as if it had been uttered by an oracle:

* *Georgics*, III:284.   † *Georgics*, III:66–8.

Life's finest days, for us poor human beings,
Fly first.

Why finest? Because what is to come is uncertain. Why
finest? Because while we are young we are able to learn;
when the mind is quick to learn and still susceptible to
training we can turn it to better ends. Because this is a good
time for hard work, for studies as a means of keeping our
brains alert and busy and for strenuous activities as a means
of exercising our bodies; the time remaining to us afterwards
is marked by relative apathy and indolence, and is all the
closer to the end. Let us act on this, then, wholeheartedly.
Let us cut out all distractions and work away at this alone for
fear that otherwise we may be left behind and only eventually
realize one day the swiftness of the passage of this fleeting
phenomenon, time, which we are powerless to hold back.
Every day as it comes should be welcomed and reduced
forthwith into our own possession as if it were the finest day
imaginable. What flies past has to be seized at.

These thoughts never occur to someone who looks at the
lines I have quoted through the eyes of our literary scholar.
He does not reflect that our first days are our best days for the
very reason that 'the sicknesses creep near', with old age
bearing down on us, hovering over our heads whilst our
minds are still full of our youth. No, his comment is that
Virgil constantly couples 'sicknesses' and 'old age' (and not
without good reason, I can tell you: I should describe old
age itself as a kind of incurable sickness). The scholar further
remarks on the epithet attached to old age, pointing out that
the poet speaks in the passage quoted of 'bleak old age' and
in another passage writes

Where dwell wan Sicknesses and bleak Old Age.*
* *Aeneid*, VI:275.

There is nothing particularly surprising about this way which everyone has of deriving material for his own individual interests from identical subject-matter. In one and the same meadow the cow looks for grass, the dog for a hare and the stork for a lizard. When a commentator, a literary man and a devotee of philosophy pick up Cicero's book *The State*, each directs his attention in different directions. The philosopher finds it astonishing that so much could have been said in it by way of criticism of justice. The commentator, coming to the very same reading matter, inserts this sort of footnote: 'There are two Roman kings one of whom has no father and another no mother, the mother of Servius being a matter on which there is uncertainty, and Ancus, the grandson of Numa, having no father on record.' He observes further that 'the man to whom we give the title Dictator and read about in the history books under the same name was called the Master of the Commons by the early Romans; this title survives to the present day in the augural records, and the fact that the person appointed by him as his deputy was known as the Master of the Knights is evidence that this is correct.' He similarly observes that 'Romulus died during an eclipse of the sun'; that 'the right of appeal to the Commons was recognized as early as the period of the monarchy; there is authority for this in the pontifical records, in the opinion of a number of scholars, in particular Fenestella.' When the literary scholar goes through the same book, the first thing he records in his notebook is Cicero's use of *reapse* for *re ipse*, and *sepse* likewise for *se ipse*. He then goes on to examine changes in usage over the years. Where, for example, Cicero uses the expression: 'Since we have been called back right from the *calx* by this interruption of his', he notes that the *calx* was the name which the old Romans gave to the finishing line in the stadium that we nowadays call the *creta*. The next thing he does is assemble lines

from Ennius, and in particular those referring to Scipio of
Africa:

> None, foe nor Roman, can assess the value
> Of his succour and do justice to his feats.*

From this passage the scholar claims to deduce that the word
'succour' to the early Romans signified the rendering not
merely of assistance but of actual services, Ennius saying that
no one, foe or Roman, was capable of assessing the value of
the services Scipio rendered Rome. Next he congratulates
himself on discovering the source from which Virgil chose to
take the following:

> Above whose head the mighty gates of heaven
> Thunder.†

He tells us that Ennius filched the idea from Homer and that
Virgil filched it from Ennius, there being a couplet of Ennius
(preserved in this very work of Cicero's I was mentioning,
The State) which reads

> If any man may rise to heaven's levels,
> To me, alone, lie open heaven's huge gates.

But enough, or before I know where I am I shall be slipping into the scholar's or commentator's shoes myself. My
advice is really this: what we hear the philosophers saying
and what we find in their writings should be applied in our
pursuit of the happy life. We should hunt out the helpful
pieces of teaching, and the spirited and noble-minded sayings
which are capable of immediate practical application – not
far-fetched or archaic expressions or extravagant metaphors
and figures of speech – and learn them so well that words
become works. No one to my mind lets humanity down quite

---

* A fragment of a lost epic.
† *Georgics*, III:260–1.

so much as those who study philosophy as if it were a sort of commercial skill and then proceed to live in a quite different manner from the way they tell other people to live. People prone to every fault they denounce are walking advertisements of the uselessness of their training. That kind of man can be of no more help to me as an instructor than a steersman who is seasick in a storm – a man who should be hanging on to the tiller when the waves are snatching it from his grasp, wrestling with the sea itself, rescuing his sails from the winds. What good to me is a vomiting and stupefied helmsman? And you may well think the storm of life is a great deal more serious than any which ever tosses a boat. What is needed is a steering hand, not talking. And apart from this, everything which this kind of man says, everything he tosses out to a thronging audience, belongs to someone else. The words were said by Plato, said by Zeno, said by Chrysippus and Posidonius and a whole host more of Stoics like them. Let me indicate here how men can prove that their words are their own: let them put their preaching into practice.

Now that I've given you the message I wanted to convey to you, I'll go on from here to satisfy that wish of yours. But I'll transfer what you wanted from me to another, fresh letter, to avoid your coming mentally weary to a subject which is a thorny one and needs to be followed with a conscientious and attentive ear.

LETTER CXIV

You ask why it is that at certain periods a corrupt literary style has come into being; and how it is that a gifted mind develops a leaning towards some fault or other (resulting in the prevalence at one period of a bombastic form of exposition, at another of an effeminate form, fashioned after the manner of songs); and why it is that at one time approval is won by extravagant conceits and at another by sentences of an abrupt, allusive character that convey more to the intelligence than to the ear; and why there have been eras in which metaphors have been shamelessly exploited. The answer lies in something that you hear commonly enough, something which among the Greeks has passed into a proverb: people's speech matches their lives. And just as the way in which each individual expresses himself resembles the way he acts, so in the case of a nation of declining morals and given over to luxury forms of expression at any given time mirror the general behaviour of that society. A luxuriant literary style, assuming that it is the favoured and accepted style and not just appearing in the odd writer here and there, is a sign of an extravagant society. The spirit and the intellect cannot be of different hues. If the spirit is sound, if it is properly adjusted and has dignity and self-control, the intellect will be sober and sensible too, and if the former is tainted the latter will be infected as well. You've observed surely, how a person's limbs drag and his feet dawdle along if his spirit is a feeble one? And how the lack of moral fibre shows in his very gait if his spirit is addicted to soft living? And how if his spirit is a lively and dashing one his step is brisk? And how if it is a prey to madness or the similar state of anger, his body moves along in an uncontrolled sort of way, in a rush rather than a walk? Isn't this all the more likely to be the case where a person's intellect is concerned, his intellect being wholly bound up with his spirit – moulded by and responsive to it and looking to it for guidance?

The manner in which Maecenas lived is too well known for there to be any need to describe the way he walked, his self-indulgent nature, his passion for self-display, his reluctance that his faults should escape people's notice. Well, then, wasn't his style just as undisciplined as his dress was sloppy? Wasn't his vocabulary just as extraordinary as his turnout, his retinue, his house, his wife? He would have been a genius if he had pursued a more direct path instead of going out of his way to avoid being intelligible, had he not been as loose in matters of style as he was in everything else. Which is why you'll notice that his eloquence resembles a drunken man's, tortuous and rambling and thoroughly eccentric. Could there be a worse expression than 'the bank with mane of stream and woods'? And look at 'men tilling with wherries the channel, driving the gardens back with the shallows' churning over'. What about a person 'curvetting at a woman's beck, with lips on billing bent, a sigh the opening of his addresses, neck lolling like a forest giant in his ecstasy'? 'The unregenerate company rummage homes for victuals, raiding them with provision jars and trading death for hope.' 'But hardly should I call as witness on his holy day my guardian spirit.' 'Else the wick of a slender waxlight and sputtering meal.' 'Mothers or wives accoutre the hearth.' When you read this sort of thing, doesn't it immediately cross your mind that this is the same man who invariably went around with casual clothes on in the capital (even when Maecenas was discharging the emperor's duties during the absence of Augustus, the officer coming to him for the daily codeword would find him in informal attire), who appeared on the bench, on the platform and at any public gathering wearing a mantle draped over his head leaving both ears exposed, looking just like the rich man's runaway slave as depicted on the comic stage? The same man whose public escort, at a time when the nation was embroiled in a civil war and the capital was under arms and in a state of alarm, consisted of a pair of eunuchs, and who went through a thousand ceremonies of marriage with his one wife?

These expressions of his, strung together in such an out-rageous fashion, tossed out in such a careless manner, constructed with such a total disregard of universal usage, reveal a character equally revolutionary, equally perverted and peculiar. Maecenas' greatest claim to glory is regarded as having been his clemency: he spared the sword, refrained from bloodshed and showed his power only in his defiance of convention. But he has spoilt this very claim of his by these monstrous stylistic frolics; for it becomes apparent that he was not a mild man but a soft one. That perplexing word order, those transpositions of words and those startling ideas which have indeed the quality of greatness in them but which lose all their effect in the expression, will make it obvious to anyone that his head was turned by overmuch prosperity.

It is a fault which is sometimes that of the man and sometimes that of the age. Where prosperity has spread luxury over a wide area of society, people start by paying closer attention to their personal turnout. The next thing that engages people's energies is furniture. Then pains are devoted to the houses themselves, so as to have them running out over broad expanses of territory, to have the walls glowing with marble shipped from overseas and the ceilings picked out in gold, to have the floors shining with a lustre matching the panels overhead. Splendour then moves on to the table, where praise is courted through the medium of novelty and variations in the accustomed order of dishes, making what normally rounds off a meal the first course and giving people as they go what they used before to be given on arrival. Once a person's spirit has acquired the habit of disdaining what is customary and regards the usual as banal, it starts looking for novelty in its methods of expression as well. At one moment it will disinter and revive archaic or obsolete expressions; at another it will coin new, unheard of expressions and give a word a new form; at another – this is something that has become very common recently – the bold and frequent use of metaphor passes for good style. There are some who cut their thoughts short and hope to win acclaim by making their meaning elusive, giving their audience a mere hint of it; there are others who stretch them out, reluctant to let them go; there are others still who do not merely fall into a defect of style (which is something that is inevitable if one is striving for any lofty effect), but have a passion for the defect for its own sake.

So wherever you notice that a corrupt style is in general favour, you may be certain that in that society people's characters as well have deviated from the true path. In the same way as extravagance in dress and entertaining are indications of a diseased community, so an aberrant literary style, provided it is widespread, shows that the spirit (from which people's words derive) has also come to grief. And in fact you need feel no surprise at the way corrupt work finds popularity not merely with the common bystander but with your relatively cultivated audience: the distinction between these two classes of critic is more one of dress than of discernment. What you might find more surprising is the fact that they do not confine themselves to admiring passages that contain defects, but admire the actual defects themselves as well. The former thing has been the case all through history – no genius that ever won acclaim did so without a measure of indulgence. Name me any man you like who had a celebrated reputation, and I'll tell you what the age he lived in forgave him, what it turned a blind eye to in his work. I'll show you plenty of stylists whose faults never did them any harm and some who were actually helped by them. I'll even say this: I could show you some men of the highest renown, men held up as objects of wonder and admiration, in whose case to amend their faults would be to destroy them, their faults being so inextricably bound up with their virtues.

Besides, there are no fixed rules of style. They are governed by the usage of society and usage never stands still for any length of time. Many speakers hark back to earlier centuries for their vocabulary, talking in the language of the Twelve Tables.* Gracchus, Crassus and Curio are too polished and modern for them. They go right back to Appius and Coruncanius. Others, by contrast, in seeking to confine themselves to familiar, everyday expressions, slip into an undistinguished manner. Both these practices, in their different ways, are debased style (quite as much so as the rejection of any expression that is not high-sounding, florid and poetical, avoiding the indispensable expressions in normal use). The one is as much a fault as the other, in my view, the first paying undue attention to itself and the second unduly neglecting itself. The former removes the hair from its legs as well, the latter not even from its armpits.

Let us turn our attention to composition. How many species of fault can I show you where this is concerned? Some like it broken and uneven, and go out of their way to disarrange any passage with a relatively smooth and even flow. They want every transition to come with a jolt, and see virility and forcefulness in a style the irregularities of which jar the ear. With some other literary figures it is not a case of composition but of setting words to melodies, so sweetly, softly do they glide along. What shall I say about the kind in which words are held back and keep us waiting for a long time before they make their reluctant appearance right at the end of the period? What of that, like Cicero's, which moves to its conclusion in a leisurely fashion, in a gentle and

* A set of tablets dating from 451–450 B.C., which record a basic code of laws and were the earliest piece of Latin writing known to the Romans.

It may be noted here that in this letter Seneca sees or draws no distinction between rules applying to literature and rules applying to oratory.

delayed incline, and unvaryingly true to its customary rhythm?

In the field of the epigram, too, faults comprise a tameness and childishness, or a boldness and daring that oversteps the bounds of decency, or a richness that has a cloying quality, or a barrenness in the outcome, an ineffectiveness, a ringing quality and nothing more.

These faults are introduced by some individual dominating letters at the time, are copied by the rest and handed on from one person to another. Thus in Sallust's heyday abruptly terminated sentences, unexpectedly sudden endings and a brevity carried to the point of obscurity passed for a polished style. Lucius Arruntius, the historian of the Punic War and a man of unusual simplicity of character, was a follower of Sallust and strove after that kind of style. 'By means of money he procured an army', hired one, in other words, is an expression found in Sallust. Arruntius took a fancy to this expression 'procured' and found a place for it on every page, saying in one passage: 'They procured our rout', in another: 'King Hiero of Syracuse procured a war', and in another: 'This news procured the surrender of the people of Panormus to the Romans.' These are merely by way of giving you samples of the practice – the whole book is rife with them. What was occasional in Sallust is of frequent, almost incessant occurrence in Arruntius, which is easily enough explained, for whereas Sallust hit on such expressions Arruntius cultivated them. You can see what the result is when some writer's fault is taken as a model. Sallust spoke of 'wintry rains'. Arruntius, in the first book of *The Punic War*, says: 'Suddenly the weather was wintry.' In another place, when he wants to describe a particular year as having been a cold one, he says: 'The whole year was wintry.' In another passage he writes: 'From there he despatched sixty transport vessels, lightly laden apart from troops and essential

crew, in spite of a wintry northerly gale.' He drags the word
in constantly, in every conceivable place. Sallust at one point
writes: 'Seeking, amid civil war, the plaudits of rectitude and
integrity'. Arruntius was unable to restrain himself from in-
serting right at the beginning of his first book mention of
Regulus' tremendous 'plaudits'.

Now these faults, and others like them, stamped on a
writer's style by imitation, are not themselves evidence of
extravagant ways or corrupt attitudes. For the things upon
which you base any judgement on a person's psychology must
be things peculiar to himself, things that spring from his own
nature, a hot-tempered man having a hot-tempered style, an
emotional man an over-excited one, a self-indulgent man a
soft and flabby one and so on. And the last is the manner one
observes adopted by the sort of person who has his beard
plucked out, or has it plucked out in parts, who keeps himself close-shaven and smooth around his lips but leaves the
rest of it to grow, who wears cloaks in flamboyant colours,
who wears a diaphanous robe, who is reluctant to do anything
that might escape people's attention, who provokes and
courts such attention and so long as he is looked at does not
mind whether it is with disapproval. Such is the manner of
Maecenas and every other writer whose stylistic errors are
not accidental but deliberate and calculated. It is something
that stems from a serious affliction of the spirit. When a
person is drinking his tongue only starts stumbling after his
mental faculties have succumbed and given way or broken
down. The same applies with this drunkenness – what else
can one regard it as? – of style. No one suffers from it unless
his spirit is unstable.

See, then, that the spirit is well looked after. Our thoughts
and our words proceed from it. We derive our demeanour
and expression and the very way we walk from it. If the
spirit is sound and healthy our style will be firm and forceful

and virile, but if the spirit tumbles all the rest of our personality comes down in ruins with it.

> The queen unharmed, the bees all live at one;
> Once she is lost, the hive's in anarchy.*

The spirit is our queen. So long as she is unharmed, the rest remains at its post, obedient and submissive. If she wavers for a moment, in the same moment the rest all falters.†

LETTER CXXII

THE daylight has begun to diminish. It has contracted considerably, but not so much that there is not a generous amount remaining still for anyone who will, so to speak, rise with the daylight itself. More active and commendable still is the person who is waiting for the daylight and intercepts the first rays of the sun; shame on him who lies in bed dozing when the sun is high in the sky, whose waking hours commence in the middle of the day – and even this time, for a lot of people, is the equivalent of the small hours. There are some who invert the functions of day and night and do not separate eyelids leaden with the previous day's carousal before night sets in. Their way of life, if not their geographical situation, resembles the state of those peoples whom nature, as Virgil says, has planted beneath our feet on the opposite side of the world

> And when Dawn's panting steeds first breathe on us,
> For them the reddening Evening starts at length
> To light their lamps.‡

* Virgil, *Georgics*, IV:212–13.
† The last 34 lines are omitted (§§23 to 27).
‡ *Georgics*, I:250–51.

There are some antipodes living in the same city as ourselves who, as Marcus Cato said, have never seen the sun rise or set. Can you imagine that these people know how one ought to live when they do not know when one ought to live? Can they really be afraid of death like other people when this is what they have retreated into in their own lifetimes? They are as weird as birds that fly by night. They may while away their hours of darkness to a background of wine and perfume, they may occupy the whole of the time they spend, contrarily, awake eating sumptuous dishes – individually cooked, too, in a long succession of different courses; but what in fact they are doing is not banqueting but celebrating their own last rites. At least the dead have their memorial ceremonies during the daytime. Heavens, though, no day is a long one for a man who is up and about! Let us expand our life: action is its theme and duty. The night should be kept within bounds, and a proportion of it transferred to the day. Poultry that are being reared for the table are cooped up in the dark so as to prevent them moving about and make them fatten easily; there they languish, getting no exercise, with the swelling taking possession of their sluggish bodies and the inert fat creeping over them in their magnificent seclusion. And the bodies of these people who have dedicated themselves to the dark have an unsightly look about them, too, inasmuch as their complexions are unhealthier looking than those of persons who are pale through sickness. Frail and feeble with their blanched appearance, in their case the flesh on the living person is deathlike. And yet I should describe this as the least of their ills. How much deeper is the darkness in their souls! Their souls are dazed and befogged, envious of the blind! What man was ever given eyes for the sake of the dark?

Do you ask how the soul comes to have this perverse aversion to daylight and transference of its whole life to the night-time? All vices are at odds with nature, all abandon the proper order of things. The whole object of luxurious living is the delight it takes in irregular ways and in not merely departing from the correct course but going to the farthest point away from it, and in eventually even taking a stand diametrically opposed to it. Don't you think it's living unnaturally to drink without having eaten, taking liquor into an empty system and going on to dinner in a drunken state? Yet this is a failing which is common among young people, who cultivate their capacities to the point of drinking – swilling would be a better description of it – in naked groups the moment they're inside the doors of the public bath-house, every now and then having a rub all over to get rid of the perspiration brought on by continually putting down the piping hot liquor. To them drinking after lunch or dinner is a common habit, something only done by rural worthies and people who don't know where the true pleasure lies: the wine that gives a person undiluted enjoyment, they say, is the wine that makes its way into his system unobstructed instead of swimming about in his food; intoxication on an empty stomach is the kind that gratifies a man.

Don't you think it's living unnaturally to exchange one's clothes for women's?* Is it not living unnaturally to aim at imparting the bloom of youth to a different period of life – can there be a sorrier or crueller practice than that whereby a boy is never, apparently, allowed to grow up into a man, in order that he may endure a man's attentions for as long as may be? Won't even his years rescue him from the indignity his sex ought to have precluded?

Is it not living unnaturally to hanker after roses during the winter, and to force lilies in midwinter by taking the requisite steps to change their environment and keeping up the

---

* Costly materials such as the silks mentioned in Letter XC, or the diaphanous robe (*perlucentem togam*) disapproved of in Letter CXIV.

temperature with hot water heating? Is it not living unnaturally to plant orchards on the top of towers, or to have a
forest of trees waving in the wind on the roofs and ridges of
one's mansions, their roots springing at a height which it
would have been presumptuous for their crests to reach? Is
it not living unnaturally to sink the foundations of hot baths
in the sea and consider that one is not swimming in a refined
fashion unless one's heated waters are exposed to the waves
and storms? Having started to make a practice of desiring
everything contrary to nature's habit, they finally end up by
breaking off relations with her altogether. 'It's daylight: time
for bed! All's quiet: now for our exercises, now for a drive,
now for a meal! The daylight's getting nearer: time we had
our dinner! No need to do as the crowd does: to follow the
common, well-worn path in life is a sordid way to behave.
Let's leave the daytime to the generality of people. Let's
have early hours that are exclusively our own.'

This sort of person is to me as good as dead. After all, how
far can a person be from the grave, and an untimely one at
that, if he lives by the light of tapers and torches?* I can recall a great many people who led this kind of life at one time,
with a former praetor among them, too, Acilius Buta, the
man who had squandered an enormous fortune which he had
inherited, and when he confessed his impoverished state to
the emperor Tiberius was met with the remark, 'You have
woken up rather late.' Montanus Julius, a tolerably good
poet, noted for his closeness to Tiberius and subsequent fall
from favour, who used to give public readings of his verse,
took great delight in working sunrises and sunsets into his
compositions. Hence the remark of Natta Pinarius when
someone was expressing disgust at the way Montanus'
reading had continued for a whole day and declaring that his
readings weren't worth attending: 'I'm quite prepared to

* Carried by custom at a child's funeral.

listen to him – can I say fairer than this – from sunrise to sunset.' When Montanus had just read the lines

> The sun god starts his fiery flames to extend,
> The rosy dawn to diffuse her light, and now
> That plaintive bird, the swallow, starts to thrust
> Her morsels down the throats of nestlings shrill,
> With gentle bill supplying each its share,
> With journeys yet to come,

one Varus called out, 'And Buta starts to sleep.' Varus was a Roman knight, a friend of Marcus Vinicius, who was always in attendance at good dinners, for which he used to qualify by the sauciness of his tongue. It was he, too, who said a little later on when Montanus had read

> The herdsmen now in byres have stalled their beasts,
> And night now starts to bring the drowsy world
> A dreamy stillness,

'What's that you say? Night, is it, now? I'll go and pay a morning call on Buta.'

Buta's upside-down way of life was a byword, and yet, as I've said, at one time this sort of life was led by a great many people. The reason why some people live in this sort of way is not that they think that night in itself has any special attraction, but that they get no pleasure out of anything which is usual; apart from the fact that daylight is anathema to a bad conscience, a person who experiences a craving or a contempt for things in proportion to their costliness or cheapness looks down his nose at a form of illumination which does not cost him anything. Moreover the man who lives extravagantly wants his manner of living to be on everybody's lips as long as he is alive. He thinks he is wasting his time if he is not being talked about. So every now and then he does something calculated to set people talking. Plenty of people squander fortunes, plenty of people keep mistresses.

To win any reputation in this sort of company you need to go in for something not just extravagant but really out of the ordinary. In a society as hectic as this one it takes more than common profligacy to get oneself talked about.

I once heard that delightful story-teller, Albinovanus Pedo, describing how he had lived above Sextus Papinius. Papinius was one of the daylight-shy fraternity. 'About nine o'clock at night I'd hear the sound of whips. "What's he doing?" I'd ask, and be told he was inspecting the household accounts. About twelve I'd hear some strenuous shouting. "What's that?" I'd ask, and be told he was doing his voice exercises. About two I'd ask what the noise of wheels meant, and be told he was off for his drive. About daybreak there would be a scurrying in all directions, a shouting for boys and a chaos of activity among stewards and kitchen staff. "What is it?" I'd ask, to be told he was out of his bath and had called for his pre-dinner appetizer. "His dinner, then," it might be said, "exceeded the capacity of his day." Far from it, for he lived in a highly economical fashion: all he used to burn up was the night.' Hence Pedo's remark when some people were describing Papinius as being mean and grasping: 'I take it you would describe him as being an artificial light addict as well.'

You needn't be surprised to discover so much individuality where the vices are concerned. Vices are manifold, take countless different forms and are incapable of classification. Devotion to what is right is simple, devotion to what is wrong is complex and admits of infinite variations. It is the same with people's characters; in those who follow nature they are straightforward and uncomplicated, and differ only in minor degree, while those that are warped are hopelessly at odds with the rest and equally at odds with themselves. But the chief cause of this disease, in my opinion, is an attitude of disdain for a normal existence. These people seek to set themselves apart from the rest of the world even in the manner in which they organize their time-table, in just the same way as they mark themselves off from others by the way they dress, by the stylishness of their entertaining and the elegance of their carriages. People who regard notoriety as a reward for misbehaviour have no inclination for common forms of misbehaviour. And notoriety is the aim of all these people who live, so to speak, back to front. We therefore, Lucilius, should keep to the path which nature has mapped out for us and never diverge from it. For those who follow nature everything is easy and straightforward, whereas for those who fight against her life is just like rowing against the stream.

LETTER CXXIII

I'VE reached my house at Alba at last, late at night and worn out by the journey (which wasn't so much long as thoroughly uncomfortable) to find nothing ready for my arrival – apart from myself. So I'm in bed, recovering from my fatigue, and making the best of this slowness on the part of the cook and the baker by carrying on a conversation with myself on this very theme, of how nothing is burdensome if taken lightly, and how nothing need arouse one's irritation so long as one doesn't make it bigger than it is by getting irritated. My baker may be out of bread, but the farm manager will have some, or the steward, or a tenant. 'Bad bread, yes!' you'll say. Wait, then: it'll soon turn into good bread. Hunger will make you find even that bread soft and wheaty. One shouldn't, accordingly, eat until hunger demands. I shall wait, then, and not eat until I either start getting good bread again or cease to be fussy about bad bread. It is essential to make oneself used to putting up with a little. Even the wealthy and the well provided are continually met and frustrated by difficult times and situations. It is in no man's power to have whatever he wants; but he has it in his power not to wish for what he hasn't got, and cheerfully make the most of the things that do come his way. And a stomach firmly under control, one that will put up with hard usage, marks a considerable step towards independence.

I'm deriving immeasurable satisfaction from the way my tiredness is becoming reconciled to itself. I'm not asking for masseurs, or a hot bath, or any remedy except time. What was brought on by exertion rest is taking away. And whatever kind of meal is on the way is going to beat an inaugural banquet for enjoyment. I have, in fact, put my spirit to a sort of test, and a surprise one, too – such a test being a good deal more candid and revealing. When the spirit has prepared itself beforehand, has called on itself in advance to show endurance, it is not so clear just how much real strength it possesses; the surest indications are the ones it gives on the spur of the moment, when it views annoyances in a manner not merely unruffled but serene, when it refrains from flying into a fit of temper or picking a quarrel with someone, when it sees to everything it requires by refraining from hankering after this and that, reflecting that one of its habits may miss a thing, but its own real self need never do so. Until we have begun to go without them, we fail to realize how unnecessary many things are. We've been using them not because we needed them but because we had them. Look at the number of things we buy because others have bought them or because they're in most people's houses. One of the causes of the troubles that beset us is the way our lives are guided by the example of others; instead of being set to rights by reason we're seduced by convention. There are things that we shouldn't wish to imitate if they were done by only a few, but when a lot of people have started doing them we follow along, as though a practice became more respectable by becoming more common. Once they have become general, mistaken ways acquire in our minds the status of correct ones. Nobody travels now without a troop of Numidian horsemen riding ahead of him and a host of runners preceding his carriage. One feels ashamed not to have men with one to hustle oncoming travellers off the road and to show there's a gentleman coming by the cloud of dust they raise. Everybody nowadays has mules to carry his crystal-ware, his myrrhine vessels and the other articles engraved by the hands of master craftsmen. One is ashamed to be seen to have only the kind of baggage which can be jolted around without coming to any harm. Everyone's pages ride along with their faces smeared with cream in case the sun or the cold should spoil their delicate complexions; one is ashamed if there is no member of one's retinue of boys whose healthy cheeks call for protection with cosmetics.

With all such people you should avoid associating. These are the people who pass on vices, transmitting them from one character to another. One used to think that the type of person who spreads tales was as bad as any: but there are persons who spread vices. And association with them does a lot of damage. For even if its success is not immediate, it leaves a seed in the mind, and even after we've said goodbye to them, the evil follows us, to rear its head at some time or other in the future. In the same way as people who've been to a concert carry about with them the melody and haunting quality of pieces they've just heard, interfering with their thinking and preventing them from concentrating on anything serious, so the talk of snobs and parasites sticks in our ears long after we've heard it. And it's far from easy to eradicate these haunting notes from the memory; they stay with us, lasting on and on, coming back to us every so often. This is why we must shut our ears against mischievous talk, and as soon as it starts, too; once such talk has made its entry and been allowed inside, it becomes a good deal bolder. Eventually it reaches the stage where it says that 'virtue and philosophy and justice are just a lot of clap-trap. There's only one way to be happy and that's to make the most of life. Eating, drinking, spending the money that's been left to you, that's what I call living – and that's what I call not forgetting that you've got to die some day, too. The days are slipping by, and life is running out on us, never to be restored. Why should we hesitate? What's the point of being wise? Our years won't always allow us a life of pleasure, and in the meantime while they're capable of it and clamouring for it, what's the point of thrusting austerity on them? Steal a march on death by disposing here and now of whatever he is going to take away. Look at you – no mistress, no boy to make your mistress jealous. Every day you go out sober. You eat as if you had to submit a daily account book to your father for approval. That's not living – that's merely being a part of the life enjoyed by other people. And what madness it is to deny yourself everything and so build up a fortune for your heir, a policy which has the effect of actually turning a friend into an enemy, through the very amount that you're going to leave him, for the more he's going to get the more gleeful he's going to be at your death. As for those sour and disapproving characters, those critics of other people's lives – and spoilers of their own – who set themselves up as moral tutors to society at large, you needn't give tuppence for them; you needn't ever have any hesitation when it comes to putting good living before a good reputation.'

These are voices you must steer clear of like those which Ulysses refused to sail past until he was lashed to the mast. They have the same power: they lure men away from country, parents, friends and moral values, creating expectations in them only to make sport out of the wretchedness of lives of degradation.* How much better to pursue a straight course and eventually reach that destination where the things that are pleasant and the things that are honourable finally become, for you, the same. And we can achieve this if we realize that there are two classes of things attracting or repelling us. We are attracted by wealth, pleasures, good looks, political advancement and various other welcoming and enticing prospects: we are repelled by exertion, death, pain, disgrace and limited means. It follows that we need to train ourselves not to crave for the former and not to be afraid of the latter. Let us fight the battle the other way round – retreat from the things that attract us and rouse ourselves to meet the things that actually attack us. You know the difference, Lucilius, between the postures people adopt in climbing up and descending a mountain; those coming down a slope lean back, those moving steeply upwards lean forward, for to tilt one's weight ahead of one when descending, and backwards when ascending, is to be in league with what one has to contend with. The path that leads to pleasures is the downward one: the upward climb is the one that takes us to rugged and difficult ground. Here let us throw our bodies forward, in the other direction rein them back.

Are you now supposing that the only people I consider a danger to our ears are the ones who glorify pleasure and inculcate in us a dread (itself a fearsome thing) of pain? No, I think we're also damaged by the people who urge us under colour of Stoic beliefs to do what's wrong. They make much of our principle that only a man of wisdom and experience can really love. 'He's the one man with a natural gift for the art of love-making, then,' they say, 'and he's equally in the best position to know all about drink and parties. Well, here's a question for discussion: up to what age is it proper to love young men?'

* Text corrupt.

This sort of thing may be all right for the Greeks, but the kind of talk to which we would be better to turn our ears is this: 'No man's good by accident. Virtue has to be learnt. Pleasure is a poor and petty thing. No value should be set on it: it's something we share with dumb animals – the minutest, most insignificant creatures scutter after it. Glory's an empty, changeable thing, as fickle as the weather. Poverty's no evil to anyone unless he kicks against it. Death is not an evil. What is it then? The one law mankind has that is free of all discrimination. Superstition is an idiotic heresy: it fears those it should love: it dishonours those it worships. For what difference does it make whether you deny the gods or bring them into disrepute?' These are things which should be learnt and not just learnt but learnt by heart. Philosophy has no business to supply vice with excuses; a sick man who is encouraged to live in a reckless manner by his doctor has not a hope of getting well.

NOTES

1. The date of Seneca's birth is not known. Scholars have tended to place it in either 5 or 4 B.C., although some have put it as early as 8 B.C. or as late as A.D. 4.

2. A procurator was a kind of commissioner or agent, as a rule mainly concerned with revenue collection, although he might hold high administrative rank. Some provinces had a procurator as their governor.

3. He wrote two handbooks on the subject for his sons. These, the *Suasoriae* and *Controversiae*, acquired a wide reputation and have survived to the present day.

4. *Antiquus rigor*, as he calls it, writing to his mother (*ad Helviam Matrem*, 17.3).

5. Letter LXXVIII.2.

6. Pliny (*Natural History*, VI:60) speaks of Seneca's work on India as mentioning 60 rivers and 118 different races – an indication of the facilities for research at Alexandria.

7. Suetonius (*Caligula*, 53) says the emperor disparagingly called him a mere 'text-book orator', his style 'sand without cement' (*arena sine calce*).

8. Dio, *Roman History*, LIX:19.

9. A fragment of Suetonius (as quoted by the scholiast on Juvenal, *Satires*, V:109) states that Seneca was exiled on the pretext of his being linked with the scandalous love affairs of Julia Livilla (*quasi conscius adulteriorum Juliae*). Dio (*Roman History*, LX:8) too speaks as if Seneca was only an incidental victim, the accusation originating in Messalina's jealousy of Julia (a sister of Agrippina, and apparently a beautiful and cultivated woman).

10. Tacitus, *Annals*, XIII:8.

11. ibid., XIII:3.

12. 'For five years Nero was so great a ruler, from the point of view of Rome's development and progress, that Trajan's frequent claim

that no emperor came near Nero in this five year period can be fully justified', to paraphrase the words of Aurelius Victor, *de Caesaribus*, 5, ii (*Nero . . . quinquennium tamen tantus fuit, agenda urbe maxima, uti merito Trajanus saepius testaretur procul differe cunctos principes Neronis quinquennio*). It should be added that not all historians are agreed that the *quinquennium Neronis* refers to the first five years of his rule.

13. *Roman History*, LXI:3.

14. *Annals*, XIII:6.

15. *Voluptatibus concessis*, by which Tacitus may be presumed to refer to the arts, sensuality and non-political cruelties.

16. *Annals*, XIII:2.

17. *Roman History*, LXI:4.

18. Grimal, *The Civilization of Rome*. Seneca's American translator, Gummere, suggests that this anomalous state of affairs may be seen as an experiment with Plato's ideal of philosopher-kingship, and one which also took account of the conditions of the time, striking a balance between the dangers of one-man rule (of which the recent reign of Caligula was a vivid illustration) and the impossibility of a return to the free elections and near anarchy of the Republic; he describes the result as a kind of cabinet system in which Seneca was the cabinet.

19. Tacitus, *Annals*, XIII:42 and Dio, *Roman History*, LXI:10 are our sources for the sort of thing that was becoming gossip.

20. *Satires*, X:16. Tacitus (*Annals*, XV:64) also used this word *praedives*, 'immensely wealthy', of Seneca, who was almost certainly a millionaire, in terms of sterling, four or five times over. Juvenal incidentally speaks of his generosity with his money as if it was well known even after he was dead (*Satires*, V:109).

21. *Roman History*, LX:32. This historian states that Seneca's sudden recall, backed by force, of enormous sums of money which he had lent to leading natives of the recently conquered province of Britain was a cause of the rising of Buduica or Boudicca ('Boadicea') in A.D. 61.

22. *Res Rustica*, III:3.3.

23. In Letters CVIII and LXXXIII, for example. In Letter LXXXVII

he describes an expedition undertaken by himself and a close friend (Caesonius Maximus, himself, a man who had had a distinguished career) in a mule-cart with the simplest of sleeping equipment and only figs or bread to eat; he speaks of having had 'a blissful two days', but regrets to report that he could not help blushing whenever they met people travelling in greater style (cf. p. 228).

24. *Roman History*, LXI: 18. Dio, usually hostile to Seneca, reports 'many reliable sources' as saying that Seneca helped incite Nero to liquidate Agrippina (*Roman History*, LXI: 12).

The murder, its significance, and the possibility (remote) of Seneca's complicity are discussed by S. J. Batomsky and P. J. Bicknell in *Theoria*, volume 19 (1962) pp. 32–6 and volume 21 (1963) pp. 42–5 (University of Natal Press).

25. *Annals*, XIV: 52f.

26. ibid., XV: 45.

27. ibid., XV: 65.

28. ibid., XV: 60–64. The passage illustrates (like the beginning of Letter CIV) the close affection between him and his young second wife. There is a rather touching mention in his treatise entitled *Anger* of how his first wife, after the light was out for the night, would keep quiet while he made his customary review of everything he had done or said in the course of the day (*De Ira*, III: 36).

29. Augustine (*De Civitate Dei*, VI: 10) says that Seneca *quod culpabat adorabat*, 'worshipped the very things he criticized'. Milton speaks of him as '*in his books* a philosopher'. La Rochefoucauld, for the frontispiece of an edition of his *Réflexions*, has him portrayed with villainous features from which a figure of Cupid representing *L'Amour de la Vérité* has just stripped a mask of virtuous amiability.

30. *Natural History*, XIV: 51.

SENECA AND PHILOSOPHY

31. Letter LXII.
32. The Stoics were considered by many as *contumaces ... ac refractarios, contemptores magistratuum aut regum eorumve per quos publica administrantur*, 'hostile to authority and resistant to discipline, disdainful of kings, magistrates or public officials' (Letter LXXIII). There are a number of cases of Stoics whose lack of respect for emperors earned them martyrdom.
33. Letter XLVIII.
34. Letter LVII. Compare Letter VI.
35. A few examples of sayings or ideas so paralleled are those of 1 *Cor.* iii, 16 (God's 'indwelling presence' – cf. Letter XLI, *init.*); 1 *Tim.* vi, 10 ('money the root of all evil'); *Job* i, 21 (we came into the world naked and go out of it naked, and '*the Lord gave, and the Lord hath taken away*'); *Rom.* xii, 5, 10 (we are members of one body, and '*Be kindly affectioned one to another with brotherly love*', etc.); *Acts* xvii, 29 (God is not like any gold or silver image); *Heb.* iv, 13 (not even thoughts are hidden from God – cf. Letter LXXXIII, *init.*); *Matt.* v, 45 (the sun rises on the wicked as well); and (as translated in the New English Bible) *Eph.* v, 1 (imitate, try to be like God). They do not lend any real support to theories that Seneca was influenced by St Paul or by Christian slaves in his own household.
36. Dr Basore.
37. Letter LXXV. Cf. 'Philosophy teaches us to act, not to talk' (Letter XX).

SENECA AND LITERATURE

38. The introduction to the translation *Four Tragedies and Octavia* by E. F. Watling (Penguin Classics) discusses generally the faults of Senecan drama and the question whether it was performable.
39. See, for example, Duff, *Literary History of Rome in the Silver Age*.
40. There are isolated passages of magnificent writing, poetic or polemic, for example in parts of Letters XC and CIV.
41. For instance in Letters XC, XCIV and XCV. The last two

incidentally (which discuss the question whether, in order to enable them to know what is the right thing to do in a given situation, people need a general 'doctrine' or a sufficient number of 'precepts', or both) are sufficient answer in themselves to critics who have said that Seneca is incapable of setting out a sustained, continuous, consistent argument. One might quote here the opinions of Coleridge: 'You may get a motto for every sect in religion, but nothing is ever thought out by him', and Quintilian: 'As a philosopher he was rather slipshod, though a magnificent censor of moral faults' (*in philosophia parum diligens, egregius tamen vitiorum insectator, Institutio Oratoria*, X:1.129).

42. In Letters CXV (e.g. *quaere quid scribas, non quemadmodum,* 'consider what, not how you should write'), C and elsewhere.

43. Duff, *Literary History of Rome in the Silver Age.*

44. *Institutio Oratoria*, X:1.125–31 forms throughout an interesting appraisal of Seneca by a famous scholar, advocate and teacher who died only thirty years or so after him. A short, late seventeenth-century comment on Seneca's style is that to be found in Aubrey's *Lives:* 'Dr Kettle was wont to say that "Seneca writes, as a boare does pisse", *scilicet*, by jirkes.'

45. *Oratio certam regulam non habet,* since fashion or usage (*consuetudo*) is constantly altering the rules (Letter CXIV).

46. Aulus Gellius, to give another example, described his language as 'trite and commonplace' (*vulgaria et protrita*), his learning as being 'of a very ordinary, low-brow character' (*vernacula et plebeia*).

47. Dante quotes him frequently and ranks him (with Cicero) after Virgil only in the *Inferno*. Chaucer, in the *Parson's Tale*, classes Seneca with St Paul, Solomon and St Augustine. Petrarch modelled his letters on Seneca's, which he knew intimately. The University of Piacenza was actually endowed with a Professor of Seneca.

48. Erasmus put many quotations from Seneca's prose works into an anthology known as the *Adagia* which has been supposed to be the source of most of the imitations or borrowings found in Elizabethan writers.

49. Montaigne (*Essays*, I:26) says 'I have never got to grips with a single solid book, apart from Plutarch and Seneca, from whom

I draw unceasingly, for ever dipping and emptying my pitcher like the daughters of Danaus' (who were set to fill a leaking jar as punishment in Hades).

Muret, his teacher, was also a devoted admirer and editor of Seneca, and Montaigne's brother-in-law, Geoffrey de la Chassaigne, made a translation of him. Lipsius, who edited (1605) and lectured on Seneca, was a correspondent of Montaigne.

50. 'She was wont to soothe her ruffled temper with reading every morning, when she had been stirred to passion at the Council, or other matters had overthrown her gracious disposition. She did much admire Seneca's wholesome advisings when the soul's quiet is fled away, and I saw much of her translating thereof.'

51. F. L. Lucas, *Seneca and Elizabethan Tragedy* (Cambridge, 1922). This book and that by T. S. Eliot mentioned below (p. 241), with *Seneca in English*, ed. Shore (Harmondsworth, 1998), will carry any interested reader well into the subject.

52. Between 1595 and 1620 his popularity rises even above Cicero's, and his influence is seen in Lyly, Nashe, Daniel, Lodge (his first English translator), Bacon, Herrick, Donne (who calls him 'that great moral man Seneca'), Ben Jonson, Henry Vaughan, Cowley, Burton, Rubens, Dryden, Pepys and Pope. G. Williamson's *The Senecan Amble* (Chicago, 1951) and R. G. Palmer's *Seneca's De Remediis Fortuitorum and the Elizabethans* (Chicago, 1953) are full of examples of Seneca's little known mark on English literature.

LETTERS

53. A lawyer's joke. Pacuvius served there for many years as deputy to a governor who was never permitted to go to his province by the emperor Tiberius. Roman law, like ours, had a doctrine of title by prescription, that is to say, the legally recognized ownership of land notwithstanding, sometimes, evidence that the occupier or 'squatter' is not the true owner, after sufficiently long occupation of it.

54. Cf. Letter LXX. 'You must not think that only great men have possessed the strength to batter down the imprisoning walls of human servitude. You must not think that this can only be done

by a man like Cato, who tore the life out of himself with his bare hands after failing to despatch it with a sword. Men of the lowliest rank have made the great effort and won deliverance; and in circumstances which did not allow them to die as and when convenient to themselves, which did not permit them any choice in the selection of the means of death, they seized on anything that came to hand and by dint of violence made weapons out of objects of a normally quite harmless nature.

'There is the recent example of one of the Germans being trained to fight beasts in the arena who, during practice for the morning show, retired to relieve himself; this was the only privacy allowed him, a guard otherwise invariably being present. In the lavatory he got hold of a rod with a sponge fixed on the end of it, put there for cleaning purposes, and stuffed the whole of it down his throat and choked himself to death. . . . Recently, again, a man was travelling on a wagon, under escort, to the morning show. He pretended to be nodding heavily with sleep and let his head drop until he was able to thrust it in between the spokes, and then hung on to his seat just long enough for the revolving wheel to break his neck, so escaping his punishment by means of the very vehicle on which he was being carried to it.'

55. Seneca here appears to misquote Virgil, who in our editions speaks of 'the phases of the moon' and not 'the stars'. Virgil's lines are actually part of a passage devoted to weather signs.

56. The story that Diogenes (the famous Cynic philosopher who lived in ostentatious poverty in Athens) slept in a *tub* no doubt dates from a time when the size of some Greek earthenware jars had been forgotten. Daedalus, in Greek mythology, was the legendary craftsman to whom all inventions could be attributed.

An Index is appended at p. 245 ff. which gives a little elementary information of possible use to those remaining curious about names or places appearing in the Letters.

FURTHER READING

C. D. N. Costa (ed.), *Seneca* (London and Boston: Routledge. and Kegan Paul, 1974, especially chapter on the *Letters* by D. A. Russell).

Dio Cassius, *Roman History* (London: Penguin Books, 1987).

T. S. Eliot, *Selected Essays* (London and Chicago: Faber & Faber, 1951, for essay on Seneca in Elizabethan translation).

M. T. Griffin, *Seneca: A Philosopher in Politics* (Oxford: Oxford University Press, 1976).

A. A. Long, *Hellenistic Philosophy: Stoics, Epicureans, Sceptics* (London: Duckworth, 1974).

F. L. Lucas, *Seneca and Elizabethan Tragedy* (Cambridge: Cambridge University Press, 1922).

H. Peter, *Der Brief in der Römischen Literatur* (Leipzig: Teubner, 1901).

L. D. Reynolds, *The Medieval Tradition of Seneca's Letters* (Oxford: Oxford University Press, 1965).

F. H. Sandbach, *The Stoics* (London: Chatto and Windus, 1975).

W. C. Summers, *Select Letters of Seneca* (London: Macmillan, 1910, especially Introduction).

W. Trillitzsch, *Seneca im literarischen Urteil der Antike* (Amsterdam: Verlag Adolf M. Hakkert, 1971).

B. H. Warmington, *Nero: Reality and Legend* (London: Chatto and Windus, 1969).

G. Williamson, *The Senecan Amble: A Study in Prose Form from Bacon to Collier* (London and Chicago: Faber & Faber, 1951).

APPENDIX

Tacitus' account of Seneca's death (Annals, XV: 60–64)

NERO asked if Seneca was preparing for suicide. Gavius Silvanus replied that he had noticed no signs of fear or sadness in his words or features. So Silvanus was ordered to go back and notify the death-sentence. According to one source, he did not return by the way he had come but made a detour to visit the commander of the Guard, Faenius Rufus; he showed Faenius the emperor's orders asking if he should obey them; and Faenius, with that ineluctable weakness which they all revealed, told him to obey. For Silvanus was himself one of the conspirators – and now he was adding to the crimes which he had conspired to avenge. But he shirked communicating or witnessing the atrocity. Instead he sent in one of his staff-officers to tell Seneca he must die.

Unperturbed, Seneca asked for his will. But the officer refused. Then Seneca turned to his friends. 'Being forbidden', he said, 'to show gratitude for your services, I leave you my one remaining possession, and my best: the pattern of my life. If you remember it, your devoted friendship will be rewarded by a name for virtuous accomplishments.' As he talked – and sometimes in sterner and more imperative terms – he checked their tears and sought to revive their courage. Where had their philosophy gone, he asked, and that resolution against impending misfortunes which they had devised over so many years? 'Surely nobody was unaware that Nero was cruel!' he added. 'After murdering his mother and brother, it only remained for him to kill his teacher and tutor.'

These words were evidently intended for public hearing. Then Seneca embraced his wife and, with a tenderness very different from his philosophical imperturbability, entreated her to moderate and set a term to her grief, and take just consolation, in her bereavement, from contemplating his well-spent life. Nevertheless, she insisted on dying with him, and demanded the executioner's stroke. Seneca did not oppose her brave decision. Indeed, loving her wholeheartedly, he was reluctant to leave her for ill-treatment. 'Solace in life was what

I commended to you', he said. 'But you prefer death and glory. I will not grudge your setting so fine an example. We can die with equal fortitude. But yours will be the nobler end.'

Then, each with one incision of the blade, he and his wife cut their arms. But Seneca's aged body, lean from austere living, released the blood too slowly. So he also severed the veins in his ankles and behind his knees. Exhausted by severe pain, he was afraid of weakening his wife's endurance by betraying his agony – or of losing his own self-possession at the sight of her sufferings. So he asked her to go into another bedroom. But even in his last moment his eloquence remained. Summoning secretaries, he dictated a dissertation. (It has been published in his own words, so I shall refrain from paraphrasing it.)

Nero did not dislike Paulina personally. In order, therefore, to avoid increasing his ill-repute for cruelty, he ordered her suicide to be averted. So on instructions from the soldiers, slaves and ex-slaves bandaged her arms and stopped the bleeding. She may have been unconscious. But discreditable versions are always popular, and some took a different view – that as long as she feared there was no appeasing Nero, she coveted the distinction of dying with her husband, but when better prospects appeared life's attractions got the better of her. She lived on for a few years, honourably loyal to her husband's memory, with pallid features and limbs which showed how much vital blood she had lost.

Meanwhile Seneca's death was slow and lingering. Poison, such as was formerly used to execute state criminals at Athens, had long been prepared; and Seneca now entreated his well-tried doctor, who was also an old friend, to supply it. But when it came, Seneca drank it without effect. For his limbs were already cold and numbed against the poison's action. Finally he was placed in a bath of warm water. He sprinkled a little of it on the attendant slaves, commenting that this was his libation to Jupiter. Then he was carried into a vapour-bath, where he suffocated. His cremation was without ceremony, in accordance with his own instructions about his death – written at the height of his wealth and power.

(*Translated by Michael Grant*)

INDEX OF PERSONS AND PLACES

Achaea, the southern part of Greece, forming a separate province of the Roman Empire, a province of which Seneca's elder brother Gallio was the governor in A.D. 50–51, 184.

Acherusian Lake, the, in Campania, 107.

Achilles, hero in the war of the Greeks against Priam's Troy; his anger with Agamemnon, the son of Atreus and leader of the Greek forces, is the foundation of the plot of Homer's *Iliad*, 152, 193.

Aegialus, a celebrated vine-grower, 148–50.

Aeneas, the hero of Virgil's epic poem, the *Aeneid*, 159.

Alba, or *Alba Longa*, an ancient place where Seneca had a country house, some twelve miles from Rome; the modern Castel Gandolfo, 226.

Alexander of Macedon or *Alexander the Great*, famous conqueror (356–323 B.C.) who carried Greek arms and culture to the farthest parts of the Middle East and even into India, 103, 143, 182.

Alexandria, founded by the above, important commercial city and centre of learning, capital of Egypt, 124.

Anacharsis, who lived in the early sixth century B.C., was one of the later so-called Seven Wise Men of antiquity; he appears to have preached the simple life later advocated by the Cynics, and to have been put to death for an attempt to introduce a Greek religious ritual into his country, Scythia (in what is now Southern Russia), 171–2.

Anacreon, a Greek lyric poet born *c.* 570 B.C., 159.

Ancus (*Ancus Martius*), early Roman king, traditionally 642–617 B.C., 210.

Antony, Mark, colleague of Julius Caesar, later ally of Cleopatra, defeated by Octavian (Augustus) at Actium in 31 B.C., 144.

Appius (*Appius Claudius Caecus*), Roman statesman, orator and first prose writer (*fl. c.* 300 B.C), 217.

Ardea, a town in a low-lying, then malarial area of Italy not far from Rome, 182, 194.

Aristotle, famous Greek philosopher (384–322 B.C.), tutor of Alexander the Great, of immense learning, author of standard works on many scientific subjects and on logic, ethics, politics and drama, 40, 119–21.

Arruntius, Lucius, Augustan senator and historian, consul 22 B.C., 218–19.

Asellius, probably *Asellins Sabinus*, Augustan literary figure and teacher of rhetoric, 85.

INDEX

THE STORY OF PENGUIN CLASSICS

Before 1946 ...'Classics' are mainly the domain of academics and students, without readable editions for everyone else. This all changes when a little-known classicist, E. V. Rieu, presents Penguin founder Allen Lane with the translation of Homer's *Odyssey* that he has been working on and reading to his wife Nelly in his spare time.

1946 *The Odyssey* becomes the first Penguin Classic published, and promptly sells three million copies. Suddenly, classic books are no longer for the privileged few.

1950s Rieu, now series editor, turns to professional writers for the best modern, readable translations, including Dorothy L. Sayers's *Inferno* and Robert Graves's *The Twelve Caesars*, which revives the salacious original.

1960s The Classics are given the distinctive black jackets that have remained a constant throughout the series's various looks. Rieu retires in 1964, hailing the Penguin Classics list as 'the greatest educative force of the 20th century'.

1970s A new generation of translators arrives to swell the Penguin Classics ranks, and the list grows to encompass more philosophy, religion, science, history and politics.

1980s The Penguin American Library joins the Classics stable, with titles such as *The Last of the Mohicans* safeguarded. Penguin Classics now offers the most comprehensive library of world literature available.

1990s The launch of Penguin Audiobooks brings the classics to a listening audience for the first time, and in 1999 the launch of the Penguin Classics website takes them online to a larger global readership than ever before.

The 21st Century Penguin Classics are rejacketed for the first time in nearly twenty years. This world famous series now consists of more than 1300 titles, making the widest range of the best books ever written available to millions – and constantly redefining the meaning of what makes a 'classic'.

The Odyssey continues ...